how2become

Police Online
Assessment Tests

ISBN: 9781912370870

First published 2020
Copyright © 2020 How2Become Ltd.

IMPORTANT: All resources, products, content, and training from How2Become is intended for educational use only, as an aid to help you prepare and come up with your own honest answers. How2Become is not acting in conjunction with, or associated with, any third-party organisation.

How2Become and its sites are not responsible for anyone failing any part of any selection process as a result of the information contained within its content, products, website, resources, and videos. How2Become and their authors cannot accept any responsibility for any errors or omissions within these resources, however, caused. No responsibility for loss or damage occasioned by any person acting, or refraining from action, as a result of the material can be accepted by How2Become.

All rights reserved. Apart from any permitted use under UK copyright law no part of this publication may be reproduced or transmitted in any form or by any means, electronic or mechanical, including photocopying, recording, or any information, storage or retrieval system without permission in writing from the publisher or under licence from the Copyright Licensing Agency Limited. Further details of such licenses (for reprographic reproduction) may be obtained from the Copyright Licensing Agency Ltd, Saffron House, 6-10 Kirby Street, London EC1N 8TS.

Get more guides, books and training courses at the website www.How2Become.com.

The police online assessment process is hard and stressful, which is why many good candidates fail it. This is why we have set up a dedicated, live webinar, presented by David Bebb, a Police recruitment expert with 30 years of experience in the MET. Our comprehensive assessment centre coaching will improve your chances of passing by increasing your knowledge, preparation, and confidence.

> **INSIDER RECRUITMENT TIPS** to ensure that you pass your police assessment, first time;

> **PROVEN INTERVIEW TRAINING** including how to tackle the competency-based interview questions and our winning template to form top-scoring answers;

> **ACCESS PRACTICE RESOURCES** so that you can prepare for the College of Policing online assessment process;

> **GET YOUR QUESTIONS ANSWERED** by a Police recruitment expert, with over 30 years of experience in helping people, just like you, to become police officers;

> **LIVE TRAINING FROM YOUR HOME** via your PC, MAC, tablet, or smartphone to ensure you get the very best coaching available & your questions get answered.

Book your place now and get 10% off using the below code.

10% OFF CODE: H2BOAP10

www.PoliceAssessmentCourse.co.uk

Contents

The Online Assessment Centre Process 7
Police Competencies and Values 23
Situational Judgement Questions 37
    Situational Judgement Questions 1 38
    Situational Judgement 1 Answers 50
    Situational Judgement Questions 2 53
    Situational Judgement 2 Answers 65
    Situational Judgement Questions 3 68
    Situational Judgement 3 Answers 80
    Situational Judgement Questions 4 83
    Situational Judgement 4 Answers 95

Written Exercises 99
    Written Exercise 1 100
    Written Exercise 1 Answers 104
    Written Exercise 2 107
    Written Exercise 2 Answers 112
    Written Exercise 3 115
    Written Exercise 3 Answers 120
    Written Exercise 4 123
    Written Exercise 4 Answers 128
    Written Exercise 5 131
    Written Exercise 5 Answers 136
    Written Exercise 6 139
    Written Exercise 6 Answers 144
    Written Exercise 7 147
    Written Exercise 7 Answers 151

Briefing Exercises 155
   Briefing Exercise 1 156
   Briefing Exercise 1 Answers 160
   Briefing Exercise 2 163
   Briefing Exercise 2 Answers 167
   Briefing Exercise 3 170
   Briefing Exercise 3 Answers 174
   Briefing Exercise 4 177
   Briefing Exercise 4 Answers 181
   Briefing Exercise 5 184
   Briefing Exercise 5 Answers 188
   Briefing Exercise 6 191
   Briefing Exercise 6 Answers 195
   Briefing Exercise 7 198
   Briefing Exercise 7 Answers 201

The Online Assessment Centre Process

Police Officer Online Assessment Tests

This chapter outlines the new College of Policing Online Assessment Process, which was first introduced in England and Wales in 2020. It is likely this online assessment process will be in place for all police constable applicants due to the COVID-19 pandemic, but please check with your own constabulary to confirm.

Within this chapter, we will look at what the online assessment will involve, the timeline for completion, how candidates will be assessed, how candidates can prepare, and some frequently asked questions on this brand-new police selection process.

WHO IS THE COLLEGE OF POLICING ONLINE ASSESSMENT PROCESS FOR?

The new online assessment process has been put together by the College of Policing as an assessment tool for police forces to use in the recruitment process of police constables/police officers.

HOW IS THE POLICE ONLINE ASSESSMENT STRUCTURED?

The new police online assessment process can be broken down into four core exercises:

1. Situational Judgement Test (SJT)
2. Video Interview (competency-based)
3. Written Exercise
4. Briefing Exercise

These exercises test the same competencies and values that are used in policing. As a candidate, you will be expected to demonstrate these competencies and values throughout these exercises.

WHAT COMPETENCIES ARE ASSESSED?

The competencies and values used in the new online police assessment centre are the same beliefs and behaviours expected of all those who work in policing.

These include the six competencies:

- Emotionally aware
- Innovative & open-minded
- Analyse critically
- Deliver, support, & inspire
- Collaborative
- Take ownership

And the four values:

- Transparency
- Integrity
- Public service
- Impartiality

You can find out more about the competencies in the next chapter.

The Police Constable selection process will only assess Level 1 of the Competencies Value Framework.

OVERVIEW OF THE POLICE SELECTION PROCESS

REGISTER INTEREST WITH A POLICE FORCE

↓

SUBMIT APPLICATION FORM AND UNDERTAKE ELIGIBILITY CHECKS

Note: Some forces will implement sifting exercises at this stage, such as a behavioural styles questionnaire and situational judgement test.

↓

POLICE ONLINE ASSESSMENT PROCESS STAGE 1:

Situational Judgement Test

Note: Police forces may use their own sifting tests, in that instance, candidates will be referred straight to Stage 2.

You MUST pass Stage 1 to move on to Stage 2.

↓

POLICE ONLINE ASSESSMENT PROCESS STAGE 2:

Video Interview (competency-based)

You MUST pass Stage 2 to move on to Stage 3.

↓

POLICE ONLINE ASSESSMENT PROCESS STAGE 3:

Written Exercise

Briefing Exercise

Note: Although both exercises make up Stage 3, you will receive invitations to these exercises separately, so they do not need to be taken together.

↓

FORCE INTERVIEW (FINAL INTERVIEW)

A structured interview to establish your values and motivation for joining the police.

Note: It is at the discretion of individual police forces if a final interview will be used. These can take place as a live video interview or may even take place in person.

Some forces will require the in-force interview to be passed before the Police Online Assessment Process stages and therefore will be conducted after the sifting tests at the start of this process.

↓

JOB FITNESS TEST, BIOMETRIC VETTING, & DRUGS TESTING

Upon successfully completing the three online assessment process stages, candidates are required to undergo a job fitness test, medical assessment, biometric vetting, pre-employment checks, non-biometric vetting, and reference check.

THE ONLINE ASSESSMENT PROCESS BREAKDOWN

Below is a breakdown of the online assessment process:

STAGE 1 - SITUATIONAL JUDGEMENT TEST

TEST LENGTH:

12 questions, approximate completion time 30 minutes to take within a maximum of 120 minutes.

The test must be completed in one session.

The test length will vary for most candidates and will be much quicker than 120 minutes to complete.

TEST OVERVIEW:

The police situational judgement test consists of 12 scenarios and questions, each containing four potential answers.

Once a question has been displayed on-screen, you will be required to select one answer from four potential answers. The answer you select should reflect what you would do in the situation described.

All of the situational judgement test questions are based on police constable scenarios.

You will not need any prior technical knowledge to complete the test, the questions are to access how you would best respond to a situation and the system will analyse if that matches with the police competencies and values.

HOW TO TAKE THE TEST:

To take the test, you will need a computer, laptop, tablet, or smartphone with a good internet connection.

You cannot take breaks during the test; it must be completed in one sitting.

You must answer every question honestly to complete the test – you cannot skip a question.

Police Officer Online Assessment Tests

HOW THE TEST IS ASSESSED:

This test measures your ability to make effective decisions which match the behaviours expected of those in the police.

This test has been developed to give candidates a look into what it's like to conduct the role of a police constable, and therefore, the answers you pick will need to reflect the same values and competencies the police use.

You will know if you have passed immediately after successfully completing the test via the system.

SAMPLE QUESTION:

This question is for demonstration purposes and is not representative of the real test, instead it is intended to give you an idea of what to expect with SJT questions.

> You are sitting in the staff canteen, when three other members from your constabulary sit down at your table. As you engage in friendly discussion with them, two of the members begin to mock the other person for his religion. Although they are only joking, you can see that the individual in question has been upset by these comments.

Select the answer option that reflects how you would react in this scenario.

1. Join in, it's just a bit of banter.

2. Speak up, and inform your colleagues that they should have more respect for other religions.

3. Ask the offended colleague to speak to you in private afterwards, where you will discuss the comments.

4. Try to change the subject.

ANSWER: *'Speak up, and inform your colleagues that they should have more respect for other religions.'*

This is the most efficient response, as you are clearly demonstrating to the affected individual that discrimination of any kind will not be tolerated, as well as challenging your colleagues on their behaviour.

STAGE 2 – VIDEO INTERVIEW (COMPETENCY-BASED)

If you are successful in Stage 1, you will be sent an email inviting you to take part in Stage 2 – the competency-based video interview.

TEST LENGTH:

The test will last up to 30-minutes and consist of five questions.

You will have one minute to view the question and then five minutes to provide your answer.

TEST OVERVIEW:

You will be required to answer five competency-based interview questions using your webcam and microphone. Your answers are recorded live by the system.

You are presented with one question at a time, along with additional information in bullet points. You have one minute to read this information. The information will also be presented to you in the form of a pre-recorded video message by an assessor.

Candidates then get five minutes to answer the question.

You will not be able to rerecord your answers.

HOW TO TAKE THE TEST:

You will need a desktop computer, laptop, tablet, or smartphone with a microphone and webcam (front camera on a smartphone) with a good internet connection.

If using a smartphone or tablet you will be required to download the College of Policing's "LaunchPad video interview" app.

You can refer to the information and material provided, but you are not allowed to take any notes or copies.

You cannot take breaks during the test; it must be completed in one sitting.

HOW THE TEST IS ASSESSED:

Candidates' answers to the interview questions will be assessed against the following competencies and values:

Values:

- Public Service
- Transparency
- Integrity

Competencies:

- Innovative and Open-mindedness
- Taking Ownership

An assessor will review and score your recorded answers after you have completed the test. You will be sent a report on how well you matched the competencies and values. If you pass, you will be invited to undertake Stage 3.

SAMPLE QUESTION:

Tell me about a time when you have demonstrated your ability to be innovative.

HOW TO ANSWER:

In this question, the interviewer is clearly testing the core competency of being innovative and open minded. So, you need to think about what these competency entails, before you can respond. Remember that being innovative and open minded requires a very specific mindset. You must be someone who is creative, can problem-solve, and is open to new methods of police work. So, try to demonstrate all of this in your response!

SAMPLE RESPONSE:

'Whilst working for my previous company, a business consultancy firm, I was one of the team leaders. Our team was specifically tasked with producing presentations for visiting clientele and customers, with the aim of endorsing our products and encouraging them to utilise our services.

On one occasion, my team was asked to make a presentation to a partnership agency who were considering investing a large amount of money in our company. This was a huge responsibility. Although I felt very nervous, I was confident in my ability to manage the team and produce a truly excellent presentation. I believed that, since I had given many similar presentations before, this one would be similar. I quickly got to work, assigning people individual roles and parts to present, based on their strengths. However, halfway through the planning, one of my colleagues pointed out to me that because of this company's particular viewpoint, it would be better for us not to present in our normal way.

Initially, this threw me a little bit. I was naturally quite happy at the idea of doing something that I was comfortable with, but I quickly realised that my colleague was correct, and changed my approach. I decided to take a completely different outlook on the project, and produce something with a bit more creative flair. I knew that this was a big risk to take, but I believed that it was the right one given the circumstances, and that our normal style of presentation would not have worked. I was happy to change my way of working, with the goal of the team in mind. When I explained my new idea to the team, they all thought it was great, and praised me for my quick innovation and on-the-spot thinking.

We got to work, and ultimately produced a brilliant presentation. The partnership agency were extremely impressed, and ultimately invested even more money than we had hoped for. As a result, my managers were full of praise for both myself and my team.'

STAGE 3 – WRITTEN EXERCISE

If you are successful in Stage 2, you will be sent two separate invitations via email inviting you to take part in Stage 3 – the first of which is the written exercise.

TEST LENGTH:

The total test time will last approximately 40 minutes.

Within this time, you will need to read all of the provided supporting information and complete the exercise.

TEST OVERVIEW:

You will undertake the role of a PC (police constable) for this task, where you are required to complete an urgent written task for your direct manager.

This task is likely to focus on an issue in the community.

You will be provided four sets of information (such as, potentially, a letter or email from a member of the public) that you can use to help form your written report.

You are required to type the written exercise on your device in your web browser.

HOW TO TAKE THE TEST:

You will need a desktop computer, laptop, or tablet with a good internet connection.

At the end of the exercise, you are required to use your webcam and microphone to record your name to verify your identity.

You cannot take breaks during the test; it must be completed in one sitting.

HOW THE TEST IS ASSESSED:

Candidates' will be assessed against the following competencies and values during the written exercise:

Values:

- Impartiality

Competencies:

- Analyse critically
- Deliver, support, & inspire
- Collaborative
- Taking ownership

It is essential that you only use the information provided and that you do not make any new information up in your report.

You are not allowed to use any external resources to aid your preparation – such as the competencies and values printed out next to you.

An assessor will review and score your written exercise after you have completed this assessment and the briefing exercise.

STAGE 3 – BRIEFING EXERCISE

The second part of Stage 3 is the Briefing Exercise. This is the final part of the police online assessment process.

TEST LENGTH:

The briefing exercise will last for a maximum of 46 minutes.

The test will be broken down into 10 minutes to prepare using the information provided and a further 36 minutes to answer the questions relating to this information.

TEST OVERVIEW:

You will undertake the role of a PC (police constable) for this task, where you are presented a scenario in which you are required to handle a series of issues.

During this exercise, you will be provided a set of questions relating to the issues from this scenario, which you must provide answers to.

You will be provided additional information and materials to aid your preparation within the first 10 minutes of the exercise.

After the preparation phase, you will have 36 minutes to present your answers broken down into the following stages:

> PART 1 – Candidates are required to answer questions relating to the first part of the scenario for 12 minutes.
>
> PART 2 – Candidates will be given further information and four new questions based on the second part of the scenario and given a total of 12 minutes to complete this stage.
>
> PART 3 – Candidates will be given further information and four new questions based on the third part of the scenario and given a total of 12 minutes to complete this stage.

ANSWERING QUESTIONS

When it comes to answering questions, you'll need to do this in the correct way. It's okay to take a moment to think before speaking, as you consider what has been asked. Don't just rush into an answer without considering the question first, because if you don't answer properly then this will show that you aren't a good listener, and that you don't pay enough attention to detail – both of which are core qualities for police constables to have!

Police Competencies and Values

Police Officer Online Assessment Tests

The UK police are now using a new set of competencies and values to evaluate candidates throughout the Online Assessment Centre.

Police Values

The police values are a key part of the basic behavioural guidelines for any police employee. As one of the most esteemed and respected organisations in the world, the UK Police naturally have a number of values that they expect all candidates and employees to abide by, along with a strong code of ethics. In the past, the police have largely focused on the competencies of candidates rather than on their values as a person. While these values were still important, they played a secondary role. Now, the police are recognising that it's extremely important to hire candidates with strong values and ethics, and the new selection process is a reflection of this.

The new police values are as follows:

Impartiality

Impartiality is all about staying true to the key principles of fairness and objectivity. It's absolutely vital that police officers can be impartial when dealing with members of the public, and with their colleagues. You must treat every single person that you meet with fairness and equal consideration, and be able to recognise and reprimand any and all forms of discrimination. Police officers must be able to put aside their personal feelings or beliefs and make decisions with clear logic and rationale.

A police officer who can act with impartiality can:

- ✓ Understand the varying needs of individuals, and take these into account when making decisions.
- ✓ Treat every person in a fair and respectful manner.
- ✓ Ensure that they communicate effectively with everyone they meet, clearly relaying the message.
- ✓ Challenge prejudice and discrimination, whenever it arises.
- ✓ Make decisions using fair and objective reasoning.
- ✓ Value and appreciate the opinions of everyone whom they come into contact with, provided they are not in contradiction with the police code of ethics.

Integrity

Integrity is another extremely important part of the police code of ethics. Police officers must be able to act with integrity and decency at all times, and be capable of recognising both good and poor performance. As a police officer, your professionalism is absolutely integral. You are a representative of the police – a role model – and therefore it's fundamental that you can present an honest and trustworthy approach to the public. By doing this, you can build confidence with the public in the police force and deliver a far more effective service.

A police officer with integrity can:

- ✓ Ensure that they behave in accordance with the police code of ethics, and make decisions that are focused on benefitting the public.
- ✓ Make decisions that will improve the reputation of the police, and understand their position as a role model within society.
- ✓ Welcome and take on board constructive criticism.
- ✓ Use their position of authority in society in a fair and professional manner, and as a force for positive change.

Public Service

The third value on the list is public service. This value again links back to the police code of ethics, and is essentially about acting with the best interests of the public in mind. The police are there to protect the public, and safeguard them from harm. Therefore, it's important that your decisions are made with this aim in mind. You must be able to evaluate different strategies, how they will be of benefit to the wider public, and take responsibility for delivering upon these. Furthermore, public service is about facing up to challenges and adversity, and overcoming these obstacles, to provide a great level of service. You must be able to engage and communicate with the public, listening to their needs and making them feel valued and appreciated.

A police officer with good public service can:

- ✓ Act with the best interests of the public in mind.
- ✓ Put the needs of the public above their own interests.
- ✓ Adapt their communication to the appropriate audience.
- ✓ Make a conscious effort to understand the needs of different members of the public.

Transparency

Transparency is a really important quality for any police officer to have. This value is closely linked with honesty. It's essentially about being someone whom others can trust and have faith in. You must be able to explain, verbally and in writing, the rationale behind your decisions. You must be genuine with everyone you are communicating with, and make a concerted attempt to build trusting and strong relationships with your colleagues. Likewise, you must be someone who is capable of accepting criticism and improving your own working practice. It's very important that you can learn from and accept your own mistakes.

A police officer with transparency can:

- ✓ Be truthful, honest and tactful with others.
- ✓ Demonstrate an honest and critical approach to their own work, accepting that there are always areas for improvement.
- ✓ Take a clear and comprehensive approach to communicating with colleagues and members of the public.
- ✓ Behave in a way that invites members of the public, and their colleagues, to trust in them and their decision making.
- ✓ Understand and maintain confidentiality.

Looking at the values, you should be able to see that these are all basic behavioural qualities that you would expect from any police officer. During the selection process, it's likely that you'll be challenged on these values – through interview questions and various exercises, so make sure you study sufficiently, learning them properly.

Competencies

Competencies are a set of behavioural characteristics that all candidates are expected to exhibit. These are behavioural qualities that you will need to demonstrate on a constant basis while working as a police officer, and therefore it's vital for the police to establish that you understand said qualities, and that you've previously demonstrated them in the past.

Emotionally Aware

It's very important for police officers to be emotionally aware. Not only do you need to be emotionally aware towards the needs and feelings of others, but you also need to be emotionally aware of yourself. You must be able to control your emotions when under high amounts of pressure, and exhibit strong levels of decision making. Police work is highly stressful, and will push you to your limits. Therefore, it's vital that police employees can stay calm and collected, and manage their emotions.

Candidates must exhibit qualities such as:

- ✓ Treating others with respect and compassion.
- ✓ Acknowledging other people's opinions, values and beliefs – provided they fall within lawful boundaries.
- ✓ Asking for help when necessary.
- ✓ Recognising their own limitations, and seeking assistance in accordance with this.
- ✓ Adapting their approach to the needs of specific/different individuals.
- ✓ Promoting diversity and valuing the different qualities of individual colleagues.
- ✓ Encouraging others to reflect on their work, and supporting them to improve.
- ✓ Taking responsibility for the emotional welfare of their team members.
- ✓ Understanding the reasons behind certain organisational behaviour requirements, and playing a key role in adapting and improving these expectations when necessary.
- ✓ Using their influence in an effective and professional manner, to help resolve internal issues within the police force.
- ✓ Viewing police work through a variety of spectrums, and being able to challenge their own views and assumptions.

Taking Ownership

It's vital that you can take ownership and responsibility, and be accountable for your own actions. This means accepting that sometimes minor mistakes will happen, but it's how you deal with these which is important. You must learn from your mistakes, and seek improvement-based feedback. It's also critical that you take pride in your work, and recognise your own limitations.

Candidates must exhibit qualities such as:

- ✓ Accurately identifying and responding to problems/issues.
- ✓ Completing tasks with enthusiasm and positivity.
- ✓ Taking responsibility for their own decisions.
- ✓ Providing others with helpful and constructive feedback on their working practice.
- ✓ Promoting an internal and external culture of ownership and responsibility, so that their colleagues can also take responsibility for their own decisions.
- ✓ Play an active role in making improvements to the police force, through regular examination of police policies and procedures, to ensure that the service is operating to its maximum potential.
- ✓ Taking accountability for the decisions that other members of their team make.
- ✓ Taking personal responsibility for correcting problems that they notice within the force.
- ✓ Embracing the idea of being a role model, and using mistakes and errors as a learning process and a chance for improvement.
- ✓ Helping to instigate measures that will allow others to take responsibility in a more effective and smooth fashion.
- ✓ Looking at issues from a wider police perspective, and how they will impact the reputation of the service as a whole.
- ✓ Being someone whom others can look up to, in order to see the excellent and all-encompassing standards and values of the UK police.

- ✓ Helping others to understand their individual goals, comprehensibly, and how these goals fit in with the wider vision of the police.
- ✓ Monitoring changes, both internally and externally, and taking steps to guarantee positive outcomes.
- ✓ Thinking in a strategic and detailed fashion, demonstrating long-term planning and knowledge.

Analyse Critically

Working as a police officer involves large amount of critical analysis. You'll be presented with a wide variety of data, and will need to use all of this data to come to informed decisions. This is essentially what 'taking an evidence-based approach' means. It's about using the evidence available to you effectively and efficiently, to gather as many facts and hard info as possible, before using this data in the most logical way.

Candidates must exhibit qualities such as:

- ✓ Understanding the importance of critical thinking, analysis and careful consideration before making decisions.
- ✓ Assessing and analysing information in an efficient and accurate manner.
- ✓ Solving problems by using logic and sound reasoning.
- ✓ Balancing the advantages and disadvantages of actions, before taking them.
- ✓ Recognising and pointing out flaws in data or information.
- ✓ Taking information from a wide range of sources into consideration, before making decisions.
- ✓ Understanding the long-term consequences of potential actions.
- ✓ Recognising when the right time to take action is, and understanding how to limit the risks involved in said action.
- ✓ Encouraging others to make decisions in line with the police code of ethics.
- ✓ Balancing out the risks and benefits of all decisions, with consideration on the wider impact of said decisions.
- ✓ Understanding when it's appropriate to raise concerns or challenge decisions made by those in a senior position to them.
- ✓ Using their knowledge of wider policing to inform their decisions.
- ✓ Being willing to make difficult decisions, even if these decisions could result in significant change.

Innovative and Open Minded

The final competency challenges the mindset of the candidate. It's extremely important that you can take an open-minded approach to police work. Not everything is straightforward and 'by the book'. There will always be problems which require an innovative and creative solution, and it's your job to come up with this solution! Furthermore, it's essential that you can take an open mind to **new** ways of working, and understand that continuous development is a necessity for any police officer.

Candidates must exhibit qualities such as:

- ✓ Being open to new perspectives, ideas and perceptions.
- ✓ Sharing ideas and suggestions with colleagues, with the aim of improving current police practice.
- ✓ Reflecting on their own working practice and how it can be improved.
- ✓ Adapting to changing circumstances and needs.
- ✓ Using a number of different sources to gain information, using common sense, and not 'just' police criteria.
- ✓ Identifying potential barriers or problems which could present an obstacle to the way in which they and their colleagues work in the future.
- ✓ Taking a flexible approach to problems, being willing to adapt and change when necessary.
- ✓ Encouraging others to think creatively, and taking risks it is correct to do so.
- ✓ Implementing new ways of working, which can have a significant, positive change on future working practice.
- ✓ Encouraging others to review their own performance through the lens of long-term policing.
- ✓ Playing a central role in developing a positive learning culture, taking steps to promote innovation and creativity.
- ✓ Taking part in creating new initiatives, with police partnership agencies.
- ✓ Taking accountability for improvement and change within the police force.

Situational Judgement Questions

Situational Judgement Questions 1

Q1. You have been called out to attend a reported theft from a convenience store. A shoplifter has been caught with several inexpensive bottles of wine in their bag. They explain that they don't have any money until pay-day, but they intended to return later in the week once they had been paid.

Do you:

a) Tell the shoplifter that they must return the stolen items to the owner of the store and that you will accompany them to the nearest alcohol support group meeting.

b) Demand the shoplifter return the stolen items then leave the store immediately, advise that they will be arrested if they return to the premises.

c) Ask the shopkeeper what action they would like to be taken against the shoplifter, reassure the shopkeeper that they will have your full support.

d) Take the shoplifter to one side and question them to gain an understanding of why they were attempting to steal the bottles of wine.

Answer | d | ✓

Q2. Your station has received multiple complaints from local residents that the children's play park is being used as a race track by local teenagers late at night. The grass is continuously being churned up and the climbing equipment is left covered in thick mud and therefore unusable.

What action would you take?

a) Arrange for nightly patrols to keep an eye on the park and move along any teenagers that enter the park after dark.

b) Inform the residents that, as no criminal activity has taken place, you are unable to assist.

c) Arrange a meeting with the local residents and encourage them to visit the park in large numbers to act as a deterrent.

d) Advise the local council that lockable gates should be installed at all entry points of the play park to prevent any further anti-social behaviour.

Answer | d | ✓

Q3. You are half an hour late leaving the station due to a huge increase in workload. As you leave at the end of a long shift a colleague approaches you and loudly berates you for not filing an important report before leaving. You know that you gave this report directly to your Sergeant one hour ago.

Do you:

a) Tell the colleague that your Sergeant has the report and that you'll make sure it's filed first thing tomorrow morning.

b) Explain to the colleague that you have, in fact, filed the report and remind him that he has no business bringing this up publicly.

c) Calmly explain that you gave the report to your Sergeant, so your colleague should take it up with him.

d) Check with your Sergeant if he requires any further action from you with regards to the report and inform him of your colleague's behaviour.

Answer   d ✓

Q4. You are on patrol in the local shopping centre. Police presence has been increased here due to the spike in shoplifting that occurs in the run up to Christmas. You receive a radio message that a group of known offenders have just entered the shopping centre and centre management are requesting you to relocate to the groups known target area - Blue Zone, second floor. As you set off you hear a man shouting and swearing at a pregnant lady, with a pushchair, at the lifts.

'I was waiting here first, you'll regret pushing in front of me once we get into the carpark.'

What action do you take?

a) Continue heading to Blue Zone on the second floor but radio the centre management to watch the aggressive man on the centre's CCTV cameras to keep an eye on him.

b) Radio centre management, alert them of the situation you have witnessed and advise you will head to Blue Zone as soon as you have resolved the altercation.

c) Approach the man and explain he must leave the centre immediately, escort him out via the Blue Zone exit so you can locate the potential shoplifters once he has left.

d) Immediately head to the carpark to make sure the woman is safe getting to her car. Once you are set up, radio management to inform them you cannot patrol Blue Zone at present and suggest another officer or security guard take over Blue Zone patrol.

Answer | b | ✓

Q5. You are working on a very important case involving a local celebrity. You're off-duty on a Saturday evening when your personal phone rings, when you answer it's a journalist from the local newspaper who offers you £50,000 for an exclusive story. They assure you will have total anonymity. The owner of the paper is very good friends with your Superintendent.

Do you:

a) Politely decline but inform the journalist they may have a better chance of getting an exclusive story if their boss calls in a favour from your Superintendent.

b) Agree to sell a story but then inform your Superintendent of what has happened so they can arrest the journalist on bribery charges.

c) Refuse to sell a story and inform your Superintendent of what has happened so they can arrest the journalist on bribery charges.

d) Decline to speak with the journalist and inform your Sergeant that you have been contacted.

Answer: d ✓

Q6. Whilst on patrol, you see a woman sitting in the doorway of a closed shop. She is asking passers-by if they will buy her cigarettes from the newsagents next door. Everyone is walking past the woman, ignoring her.

Do you:

a) Leave the woman to it, clearly no-one is bothered by her presence and she isn't doing anything wrong.

b) Reprimand the next person you see who ignores her and question them on their lack of community spirit.

c) Explain to the woman that begging is a criminal offence and suggest she moves on or else you will have to arrest her.

d) Ask the woman if she would like you to buy her a drink and hot lunch from the nearby bakery.

Answer   c ✓

Police Officer Online Assessment Tests

Q7. You're wrapping up a tough case where you have thankfully reunited a missing teenager with his parents. You've put in many extra hours to achieve this positive outcome and whilst you are pleased, you feel exhausted. As you're leaving the station the mother of the teenager approaches you and hands you an envelope containing £1,000 in cash. She explains that no-one worked harder to find her son than you and she wants you to accept this gift from her and her family. Your station has a strict policy of not receiving monetary gifts.

Do you:

a) Thank the woman, accept the cash, then hand it to your supervisor so the money can be used to increase the stations funding.

b) Thank the woman, but politely decline. Explain that you were just doing your job and that the gesture is not necessary.

c) Thank the woman, explain that you are unable to accept a cash gift but everyone at the station likes the local fish and chip shop and ask if she'd like to buy everyone dinner instead.

d) Thank the woman for the gesture but explain that this money would be better utilised by a charity who are dedicated to helping runaway teenagers so you would not feel right accepting it.

Answer b ✓

Q8. You're on patrol with a new constable when you see a group of men loudly cheering and singing. They've just left a local football match where their team have won. Your fellow constable tells you that one of the men used to bully him at school, and now he's going to get revenge by arresting him for anti-social behaviour, citing the noise the group is making as evidence.

Do you:

a) Tell the constable that this will be an abuse of power and you will report him to his supervisor if he follows through with his threat.

b) Approach the group of men together, when your colleague begins the arrest, explain that there has been a mistake, no crime has been committed and allow the men to continue their celebrations.

c) Sympathise with the constable, but firmly explain that would be unacceptable and you will have no part in it.

d) Explain to the constable that no crime has been committed but you can follow the group of men and wait and see if they demonstrate any behaviour that would warrant an arrest.

Answer: a ✓

Q9. The local community has seen a recent spike in distraction burglaries, multiple reports have been received whereby a man has been gaining access to properties claiming to have been sent by the council to check the properties water pressure. All of the victims have then found cash, jewellery and other valuables missing. The council have confirmed they do not send agents out without confirming an appointment date and time first.

Which course of action will you recommend:

a) Arrange a meeting with the local Neighbourhood Watch to discuss prevention methods which can be utilised to avoid falling victim to this type of crime.

b) Send out leaflets to all residents reminding them not to allow access to any unknown caller they are not expecting and to always request to see an ID.

c) Arrange for the council to send a letter to all residents to alert them of the burglaries and recommend safety advice to prevent falling victim to such scams.

d) Ensure that the council remind their workers to verify all appointments with customers prior to arrival and always show ID before entering the property.

Answer: C ✓

Q10. You have been called to a Primary School to resolve an issue between two mums who have been engaging in verbal conflict every day after school. After a brief conversation with the women it is apparent that Mum 1 believes Mum 2 is "an idiot" for only giving her child vegetarian food for their packed lunch. Mum 1 claims that the child will have stunted development due to a lack of meat in their diet.

What do you recommend to diffuse the situation:

a) Advise Mum 1 to avoid public disagreements and to raise any concerns they have for the child's wellbeing to the school's headteacher.

b) Tell Mum 2 not to engage with Mum 1 and to ignore any further unwarranted opinions she receives.

c) Discuss the problem with the headteacher and recommend the children are collected from separate playgrounds to prevent the mums seeing each other.

d) Remind both women that a healthy, balanced diet is imperative for children and this can be achieved many different ways. Tell Mum 1 that her comments are baseless and she should desist immediately.

Answer | d | X

Q11. It's Friday afternoon and you are attending the scene of a road traffic accident. A young man on a motorcycle has collided with a car and is being airlifted to a specialist hospital. The man's mother is at the scene and she tells you that her son is a promising young footballer and has a trial with a national team next week.

The paramedics on scene have advised you that the man has suffered serious ligament damage in his knee and have asked you to relay this information to the mother.

What do you do:

a) Ask the paramedics to tell the mother, they have more medical knowledge than you and are better equipped to explain the injury and consequences.

b) Tell the man's mother he may not be able to attend his trial but ensure her that the medical personnel will keep her up-to-date with any developments.

c) Explain to the mother that there is ligament damage to her son's knee which will likely result in the end of his football career.

d) Gently disclose the type of injury to the mother but do not mention any impact this may have on his life or career.

Answer | b | X

Q12. You are preparing to take a statement from a witness to a robbery in the town centre. Upon entering the room, the witness shows a clear disdain towards you. As you set up your equipment he suddenly exclaims 'I would be more comfortable speaking to a male officer, I cannot trust a woman to understand what I'm going to tell you and it's imperative that the perpetrator is caught. Fetch a male officer immediately or this meeting won't go ahead'.

How do you respond?

a) "Okay sir, in that case I would like to politely ask you to leave the premises."

b) "Let me check when a male officer will be available, I cannot guarantee anyone will be free to speak with you for another couple of hours though so you will have to wait".

c) "Please be assured that I am more than competent to take your statement and I am as keen as you to find the suspect and get justice for the victim."

d) "If you would be more comfortable with a male officer I will try and find someone to sit in with us. However, I am able to take your statement without assistance and I am very keen to hear what you know about this incident."

Answer [d] ✓

Situational Judgement 1 Answers

Q1. c) Ask the shopkeeper what action they would like to be taken against the shoplifter, reassure the shopkeeper that they will have your full support.

This is the most suitable course of action because this person may steal from another shop once they leave so it must be addressed immediately and it's also important to make sure the shop owner feels supported.

Q2. d) Advise the local council that lockable gates should be installed at all entry points of the play park to prevent any further anti-social behaviour.

This is the most suitable course of action because its effectively deals with the problem in the most efficient manner.

Q3. d) Check with your Sergeant if he requires any further action from you with regards to the report and inform him of your colleague's behaviour.

This is the most suitable course of action because by checking with your Sergeant you are able to confirm that the report is complete and whether it has been filed already or if any further action is required from you.

Q4. b) Radio centre management, alert them of the situation you have witnessed and advise you will head to Blue Zone as soon as you have resolved the altercation.

This is the most suitable course of action because you are prioritising an incident that is already happening and needs to be resolved over a potential shoplifting which has not yet happened. You are also promptly letting the Centre Management know that you are unable to immediately attend Blue Zone so they can respond accordingly.

Q5. d) Decline to speak with the journalist and inform your Sergeant that you have been contacted.

This is the most suitable course of action because it would not be appropriate in any circumstances to engage with the journalist regarding any case and your Sergeant should be given a factual account of what has happened, without opinion.

Q6. c) Explain to the woman that begging is a criminal offence and suggest she moves on or else you will have to arrest her.

This is the most suitable course of action because although it is impassive the woman should be not begging.

Q7. b) Thank the woman, but politely decline. Explain that you were just doing your job and that the gesture is not necessary.

This is the most suitable course of action because there should not be any exception to the station's no-monetary gift policy regardless of the level of work undertaken.

Q8. a) Tell the constable that this will be an abuse of power and you will report him to his supervisor if he follows through with his threat.

This is the most suitable course of action because you are challenging the constable's unprofessional behaviour and reinforcing this by making him aware you will report the behaviour should he carry out his threat.

Q9. c) Arrange for the council to send a letter to all residents to alert them of the burglaries and recommend safety advice to prevent falling victim to such scams.

This is the most suitable course of action because the council will be able to swiftly post out letters to all residents. Also, it's important that residents are not only advised how to notice distraction burglars and what steps to take to protect themselves, but also that they are made aware of the increase of these types of crimes in their local area.

Q10. c) Discuss the problem with the headteacher and recommend the children are collected from separate playgrounds to prevent the mums seeing each other.

This is the most suitable course of action because whilst this is a situation which does not require your opinion on which foods their children should have for lunch, both mums are entitled to their own opinions. To avoid insults being thrown and undesirable behaviour on the playground the most effective solution is to have them collect their children from separate areas of the school.

Q11. d) Gently disclose the type of injury to the mother but do not mention any impact this may have on his life or career.

This is the most suitable course of action because you do not have the medical training to discuss the man's prognosis beyond the details provided by the paramedics.

Q12. d) "If you would be more comfortable with a male officer I will try and find someone to sit in with us. However, I am able to take your statement without assistance and I am very keen to hear what you know about this incident."

This is the most suitable course of action because you are acknowledging the man's request to have a male officer whilst confirming that you are ready and able to take the statement yourself.

Situational Judgement Questions 2

Q1. You're policing a local fundraising event and you have been assigned to assist on the doors with bag searches. The event has been a huge success and tickets sold out within one hour. Whilst conducting a search, you overhear a visitor shouting at a member of staff.

Visitor: 'I've shown you my ticket, now let me in immediately!'

Staff member: 'Ma'am, I'm very sorry but this ticket is only valid for yesterday's date. You will need a valid ticket for today to enter.'

Visitor: 'Are you stupid? I've paid good money to attend this event, if you don't let me in right now I'll make sure the fund-raisers know you were trying to scam me out of more money! Probably so you can pocket it yourself!'

At this point you decide to step in.

a) Check the woman's ticket, confirm that her ticket is not valid for today's event and advise that no further tickets are available. Unfortunately she will not be permitted entry to today's event.

b) Tell the woman that although her ticket is, in fact, for yesterday's event she can enter. After all, it's for charity!

c) Ask to see the woman's ticket and confirm that she has arrived a day late for the event she booked and paid for. Advise she contacts the fundraiser's organisers to see if they are able to assist.

d) Request the woman refrains from shouting at the member of staff, confirm that the ticket she has presented is not valid for today's event. Express that you understand how frustrated she must be, but it may not be possible to admit her entry today.

Answer: d

Q2. Whilst on patrol on a busy Friday night, you receive a radio message to assist with an altercation outside a new club. When you arrive, two men are clearly very agitated though they are being kept apart by helpful members of the public.

Man 1: 'If I see you anywhere near my girl again, you'll regret it.'

Man 2: 'Yeah, sure mate. What are you gonna do about it?'

Do you:

a) Arrest Man 2, he is antagonising the situation and will likely escalate the situation further if given the opportunity.

b) Speak to both men separately to ascertain exactly what has happened.

c) Advise Man 1 to re-enter the club with his girlfriend and advise Man 2 to either go to another club or go home, but explain he is not to return to this location.

d) Ask the club's management what they would like you to do.

Answer: b ✓

Q3. Your Sergeant has assigned you to prepare a workshop for the local secondary school. Recently, members of the community have been voicing their lack of trust in the police due to a number of unsolved crimes, including a string of burglaries at a new-build estate, as well as vandalism in Ficshire Park. You are deciding what you want to focus the workshop on.

Do you choose to:

a) Use the workshop to find out what the school children know about the burglaries and vandalism - there's a good chance they might know who's responsible for these crimes.

b) Focus the workshop on the good work the police have done recently and use the opportunity as a recruitment information workshop.

c) Use the workshop to find out how the school children would like you to resolve the unsolved burglaries and vandalism.

d) Create an informative workshop detailing the process for investigating crimes such as burglary or vandalism, advise the school children how they can contact the police with information about a crime.

Answer: d ✓

Q4. You are working an extra shift, covering for a colleague on her usual patrol. It's not an area you are too familiar with but you're with another constable who is familiar with the patrol. You notice a group of teenagers congregating under a seating area, the other constable tells you they've caught many drug deals going on at this seating area.

Do you:

a) Continue your patrol, there is no clear evidence a drug-deal is occurring at the moment.

b) Continue your patrol but loop back around in a few minutes to keep an eye on the group.

c) Approach the group in a friendly manner, ask them how they are and what they are doing.

d) Approach the group and inform them to disperse from the seating area.

Answer | C | ✓

Q5. You are assisting with a roadside vehicle check operation. Your instructions are to pull over every fifth car to inspect that the car is roadworthy and free of obvious faults, as well as checking the driver has a valid license. The next car due for you to pull over is a brand new convertible sports car, the head of the operation whispers to you to let that car through, but pull over the car behind it, which is an old, beat-up looking truck.

Do you:

a) Follow instructions, let the convertible through and pull over the truck for a check.

b) Agree to let the convertible through and check the truck instead, but file a complaint against the head of the operation once you return to the station.

c) Pull over the convertible as per the instructions given and carry out each of the checks required.

d) Explain that you are going to check the convertible because that is the order you were given for this operation.

Answer | d | ✓

Q6. After an increase in crime in and around Ficshire train station you are assisting rail staff by providing a police presence and being a point of contact for travellers. A man approaches you and tells you that an elderly man stole his bag whilst he was getting a coffee from the cafe.

Do you:

a) Ask both men to accompany you to the ticket office where you will review the CCTV footage for the platform to determine who the bag belongs to.

b) Question both men independently about the bag to determine who it belongs to.

c) Retrieve the stolen bag from the elderly gentleman and return it to the man, inform the older man that he must leave the station's premises.

d) Ask both men to describe the contents of the bag to conclude who it belongs to, then remove whomever is in the wrong from the station.

Answer: a ✓

Q7. You are on a routine patrol with your partner, driving around Ficshire. So far your day has been uneventful and you're enjoying catching up with your colleague about your football team's latest win. Distracted, you fail to notice you are driving in a bus lane during restricted hours. You safely exit the bus lane but a penalty charge will almost certainly be issued as the bus lane has a number of cameras.

Do you:

a) Ask your colleague how he feels about saying you were responding to an incident and had to use the bus lane to get past traffic.

b) Wait to see if the penalty charge is issued, if it is apologise for your mistake and pay the fine.

c) Alert your Sergeant of what has happened, explain why you were distracted and offer to pay the fine.

d) Upon returning to the station, tell your Sergeant you unintentionally drove in a bus lane, apologise for this and tell them that you will pay the fine.

Answer: C ✗

Q8. Operation Miner is drawing to a close. You and your team have successfully identified and dismantled a huge drug-smuggling gang and the final step is a raid on the nearby apartment building where many of the known suppliers live. The entire building has been evacuated whilst a search is conducted on the homes of the suppliers. You are manning the entrance to the building to ensure no-one re-enters when a young girl approaches you and explains her bus pass is still in her apartment and she will be late for her shift as an A&E nurse if she cannot collect it now to catch the next bus.

Do you:

a) Escort the woman to her apartment to retrieve her bus pass.

b) Apologise to the woman but advise no-one is allowed back inside the building at present.

c) Refuse re-entry to the building but offer to give the woman some change for the bus.

d) Advise the woman to find your Sergeant to ask if she is allowed back into the building.

Answer   b   ✓

Q9. Whilst on patrol with a fellow constable, you notice a group of teenagers acting suspiciously at a bus stop. Upon approaching there is no evidence of any wrong-doing on their part and they explain they are just waiting for the number 14 bus, which is due in around 10 minutes. You leave the group and as you continue your patrol, your fellow colleague tells you he is familiar with the teenagers and is certain they were hiding something. He then uses racial slurs in reference to the teenagers.

Do you:

a) Challenge your colleague on his language and decide to stay nearby to keep an eye on the teenagers.

b) Contact your supervisor to report your colleague's behaviour.

c) Explain to your colleague that the language he used is unacceptable and then report this back to your supervisor upon your return to the station.

d) Stay in the area to ensure the teenagers do get on the number 14 bus, then request not to work with this constable again.

Answer [C] ✓

Q10. You are assisting at the site of a road traffic accident on the motorway, all lanes have been closed for half an hour whilst emergency services attempt to extract a woman from a car that has collided into the central reservation. Many people have got out from their cars with a couple trying to approach the emergency service vehicles. A young man suddenly exits his vehicle and charges towards you.

'You need to open at least one of these lanes right now. I've just finished a 14-hour shift, I'm tired and hungry. If you don't start letting us through now I'll report you for keeping me trapped on a motorway'.

How do you respond?

a) 'I am sorry Sir, we are dealing with a very serious incident, you should consider yourself lucky that you will get to go home'.

b) 'I do appreciate that it's frustrating having to wait but the emergency service personnel are trying very hard to save this lady's life, so I will ask you to be patient whilst we continue working'.

c) 'I am very sorry for the delays Sir, but for the safety of yourself and everyone else you must return to your car immediately'.

d) 'I understand and I am very sorry about the delay, I am hoping we can reopen at least one lane in the next 10 minutes but unfortunately I cannot promise anything'.

Answer: b ✗

Q11. You are the first responder, along with your Sergeant, to a reported robbery at the site of a small independent jewellers. You assist with taking a list of the remaining inventory. A beautiful set of diamond earrings with a matching necklace are located and logged. When you check over the inventory, before handing it over to the officer in charge of storing the evidence, you notice that the necklace is listed but not the earrings.

Do you:

a) Find your Sergeant and ask if he forgot to also list the earrings on the inventory form.

b) Hand over the form but add an addendum at the bottom describing the earrings that were found and explain they are part of a set with the necklace.

c) Ask the officer in charge of storing the evidence if you can check the bagged items as you believe some jewellery has been omitted.

d) Before submitting the inventory form, inform a superior officer that you believe the form is inaccurate and an item is missing.

Answer | d | ✓

Q12. You have been working on a covert operation - Operation Blaze - for several weeks and the latest intel has identified a secluded building as a point of interest. You have been instructed to immediately attend the location and monitor the building while a team is assembled to infiltrate. Around four miles from the destination you approach a recent road traffic accident where a car has been abandoned after colliding with a lamp post.

Do you:

a) Radio an alert to report the abandoned car but continue to the destination as instructed.

b) Radio to request a new dispatch is sent to the location of the secluded building so you are able to concentrate on making the site of the car accident safe and begin taking notes of the incident.

c) Pull over to the site of the crash, cordon off the car for the safety of the public and then check the immediate area for signs of any casualties.

d) Radio an alert to report the accident, advise you are currently en route to a location as part of Operation Blaze but you can stay at the site of the accident if another constable can be sent to the destination in preparation for the team.

Answer: a ✓

Situational Judgement 2 Answers

Q1. d) Request the woman refrains from shouting at the member of staff, confirm that the ticket she has presented is not valid for today's event. Express that you understand how frustrated she must be, but it may not be possible to admit her entry today.

This is the most suitable course of action because you are being assertive and telling the woman the way she is conducting herself is not appropriate, whilst also empathising with her situation.

Q2. b) Speak to both men separately to ascertain exactly what has happened.

This is the most suitable course of action because it's important that you give both parties a fair chance to explain their side of story. This will also provide you with a more rounded view of the situation.

Q3. d) Create an informative workshop detailing the process for investigating crimes such as burglary or vandalism, advise the school children how they can contact the police with information about a crime.

This is the most suitable course of action and is a perfect example of demonstating the core competency 'deliver, support, and inspire'.

Q4. c) Approach the group in a friendly manner, ask them how they are and what they are doing.

This is the best course of action because by taking a non-confrontational approach you will be able to build a rapport with the group if there is no wrong-doing. You will also have the opportunity to respond accordingly if you have reason to believe they are using or distributing drugs.

Q5. d) Explain that you are going to check the convertible because that is the order you were given for this operation.

This is the most suitable course of action as you must follow the orders of the operation and not act in a discriminatory manner. This also demonstrates the value 'integrity' and 'impartiality'.

Q6. a) Ask both men to accompany you to the ticket office where you will review the CCTV footage for the platform to determine who the bag belongs to.

This is the most suitable and fair way to respond to the situation as the CCTV footage should prove, indisputably, who the bag belongs to and will confirm if a theft has taken place.

Q7. d) Upon returning to the station, tell your Sergeant you unintentionally drove in a bus lane, apologise for this and tell them that you will pay the fine.

This is the most suitable course of action because you are apologising and taking ownership of your mistake.

Q8. b) Apologise to the woman but advise no-one is allowed back inside the building at present.

This is the most suitable course of action because you have instructions to refuse re-entry to the building.

Q9. c) Explain to your colleague that the language he used is unacceptable and then report this back to your supervisor upon your return to the station.

This is the most suitable course of action because you must challenge the behaviour displayed by your colleague, and you have already determined that the teenagers are not doing anything wrong.

Q10. c) 'I am very sorry for the delays Sir, but for the safety of yourself and everyone else you must return to your car immediately'.

This is the most suitable course of action because it would not be appropriate to divulge any information regarding the road traffic accident and it is very important that all other road-users remain in their cars.

Q11. d) Before submitting the inventory form, inform a superior officer that you believe the form is inaccurate and an item is missing.

This is the most suitable course of action because you know there is an item missing from the inventory form and this must be checked and rectified before the form is submitted.

Q12. a) Radio an alert to report the abandoned car but continue to the destination as instructed.

This is the most suitable course of action as you have received an instruction to immediately attend the site of the building. As this is a covert operation, there may not be anyone else who can be dispatched if you do not attend.

Situational Judgement Questions 3

Q1. You've been given a pile of paperwork that has amassed throughout the week. It needs to be organised and filed by 3pm so the logs can be updated. At 2:45pm you realise you've mis-filed several documents due to a typo made by the officer who gave you the paperwork.

Do you:

a) Try to refile the documents correctly within the next 15 minutes.

b) Find the officer who gave you the paperwork, explain that some documents have been filed incorrectly due to the typo and request an extension to refile them.

c) File the remaining paperwork then find your Sergeant and explain another officer's typo has resulted in some paperwork being incorrectly filed.

d) Immediately find your Sergeant, explain you cannot meet the 3pm deadline and ask what you should do?

Answer

Q2. You're on patrol, walking through Ficshire Park when you notice a group of teenagers from the local secondary school. One of the teenagers looks upset and is picking up items that have fallen out of their rucksack from the ground.

Do you:

a) Approach the group, ask what they are doing and suggest they leave the park.

b) Help the teenager who is picking up their belongings and ask if anyone in the group is picking on them.

c) Keep an eye on the group whilst continuing your patrol.

d) Follow the group around the park until they leave.

Answer

Q3. You're heading back to the station at the end of your patrol when you notice a man leaning into a car window that has been smashed. The car is parked on a drive and there's lots of glass on the floor. You can't see anyone else nearby.

Do you:

a) Radio for backup as you prepare to arrest the man for theft from a motor vehicle.

b) Approach the man and enquire what he is doing.

c) Wait and see what the man does, when he climbs back out the window, confront him.

d) Radio to request someone to come and investigate whilst you continue your patrol.

Answer

Q4. You have been dispatched to attend the scene of a reported assault. Upon arrival you realise the person accused of assault used to bully you relentlessly at school. Seeing them again makes you very uncomfortable. They are shouting, protesting their innocence but many witnesses have confirmed they witnessed the suspect push over an elderly lady as she was 'walking too slowly'.

Do you:

a) Detain the suspect whilst you begin collecting witness statements from bystanders.

b) Explain your relationship with the suspect and ask a colleague if they can handle this for you.

c) Place the suspect under arrest, explain to them that karma is unavoidable.

d) Ask the elderly lady if she would like to formally pursue compensation from the offender.

Answer

Q5. The booking-in system at your station has been used for the past decade. Recently you've heard your colleagues grumbling about how even though the system works, it's a convoluted process that no one likes doing.

Do you:

a) Encourage your colleagues to accept that as the system works sufficiently they should focus on the positives.

b) Arrange a meeting with all members of staff who use the system to discuss what ideas they have for improvements that could be made to the system.

c) Check if there is any training available that could help your colleagues understand how to use the system more efficiently.

d) Support your colleages and advise they speak, collectively, to your Sergeant to request a new system.

Answer ☐

Q6. Whilst assisting at a local event, you notice a commotion. Two opposing political parties have been running smear campaigns against each other. Several of the members are now involved in a public conflict which is gathering a lot of attention. You personally believe that the leader of one-side is being treated very unfairly and you agree with much of what they say.

Do you:

a) Instruct the party that opposes your personal beliefs to cease immediately or action will be taken against them.

b) Inform both parties that if they cannot be amicable whilst at the same event then both of them will be instructed to leave.

c) Take no action, they are not committing any offences at the moment.

d) Ask the leader of the party you align with if they would like your assistance to resolve the conflict.

Answer

Q7. You are due to give evidence as part of a trial. Once you receive the date you realise it is during a week you have booked annual leave for a romantic anniversary get-away. Your holiday has been booked for 7 months and is non-refundable.

Do you:

a) Decline to attend court to give evidence but offer to assist once you return if the trial is on-going.

b) Try to reschedule your holiday for a date after the trial has concluded.

c) Explain to your Sergeant that your annual leave has been booked for over 6 months and ask if someone else can attend.

d) Attend the trial date, then leave immediately for your holiday.

Answer

Q8. A mobile phone and wallet have been handed in after being left on a bus. The owner arrives to collect them and upon checking the wallet they tell you that it contained £50 in £10 notes, which is now missing.

Do you:

a) Explain to the owner that you were not aware of any cash in the wallet when it was handed in but you are happy to provide them with a description of the person who found it.

b) Apologise to the owner and offer to search the premises to see if any cash has fallen out of the wallet.

c) Explain that the wallet and phone have been stored securely since they were handed in, but if they wish to pursue the missing money they will have your full cooperation.

d) Suggest the owner contact the bus company to see if they can offer any advice.

Answer [ ]

Q9. A peaceful protest has been arranged, you have been requested to attend to provide a police presence. Some of your colleagues are concerned about their safety when attending an event like this.

Do you:

a) Empathise with your colleagues but explain they have a duty to perform.

b) Alert your Sergeant to the officer's who are reluctant to attend the protest so they can handle any concerns.

c) Discuss the concerns your colleagues have and as a group work to alleviate these so everyone is comfortable before you have to attend the protest.

d) Ask around to find any other officers who would be willing to attend the protest.

Answer

Q10. You hear a radio alert for an incident in an area that is notoriously unsafe. You don't want to attend this call and neither does your colleague.

Do you:

a) Ignore the radio alert for this call but make sure you're free to attend the next one.

b) Radio to confirm that you've received the message but ask if someone else can attend.

c) Confirm that you are responding to the call but ask for backup to be prepared to assist.

d) Leave the decision for your colleague to make.

Answer

Q11. You and a colleague are taking a statement from a witness in relation to vandalism of private property, they have provided an excellent description of the appearance of the offender. They claim they actually know the offender's name as it is a local boy who lives a few streets away. Once you have completed the form your colleague tells you that the name of the person you've been given is their cousin, he's on license and will go back to prison for a long time if he gets in any more trouble. He begs you to redact the name that the witness provided.

Do you:

a) Rewrite the report and leave out the name. There's not enough evidence yet to justify including it.

b) Explain to your colleague that it would be unethical for you to not include this information just because they know the offender so you will submit the statement as it is.

c) Sympathise with your colleague that they are in an unfortunate position but you cannot do what they're asking. When you file the statement, alert your Sergeant to the request your colleague made.

d) Refuse to delete the name from the statement, file a complaint against your colleague when you return to the station for gross misconduct.

Answer [ ]

Q12. A new store has opened up in Ficshire Town Square which specialises in halal foods. The storefront has been vandalised multiple times and they receive constant prank calls which is affecting their business. The store owner has asked for you to educate the community and put a stop to the abuse they have been receiving.

Do you:

a) Suggest the store installs CCTV which can be monitored to identify the person/s responsible for the vandalism.

b) Organise an event for the community which highlights the importance of accepting a variety of cultures within society and the consequences for crimes such as vandalism.

c) Create an informative handout to be sent to the local residents to alert them to the crimes and also inform them what halal food is and why the store is needed within the Town Square.

d) Increase patrols in and around the Town Square to act as a deterrent to potential vandals.

Answer [ ]

Situational Judgement 3 Answers

Q1. b) Find the officer who gave you the paperwork, explain that some documents have been filed incorrectly due to the typo and request an extension to refile them.

This is the most suitable course of action because you are taking ownership of the situation and ensuring the paperwork is filed correctly.

Q2. b) Help the teenager who is picking up their belongings and ask if anyone in the group is picking on them.

This is the most suitable course of action because it demonstrates both emotional awareness and public service.

Q3. b) Approach the man and enquire what he is doing.

This is the most suitable course of action because your first step should be to clarify the situation without jumping to any conclusions.

Q4. a) Detain the suspect whilst you begin collecting witness statements from bystanders.

This is the most suitable course of action because you must remain impartial and separate the alleged actions of the offender from your past experience with them. You must be able to carry out your duties professionally, even in problematic circumstances.

Q5. b) Arrange a meeting with all members of staff who use the system to discuss what ideas they have for improvements that could be made to the system.

This is the most suitable course of action as this demonstrates innovation, open-mindedness, and the ability to analyse critically.

Q6. b) Inform both parties that if they cannot be amicable whilst at the same event then both of them will be instructed to leave.

This is the most suitable course of action because you must show impartiality, regardless of your own personal views and beliefs. If both parties are behaving inappropriately they must be managed equally.

Q7. b) Try to reschedule your holiday for a date after the trial has concluded.

This is the most suitable course of action, as although it may be inconvenient for you plans, your evidence may be vital in the trial and if your holiday is rescheduled you will be able to dedicate your full attention to the trial.

Q8. c) Explain that the wallet and phone have been stored securely since they were handed in, but if they wish to pursue the missing money they will have your full cooperation.

This is the most suitable course of action as although you are not aware of any cash in the wallet it's possible a theft has occurred and this must be treated seriously.

Q9. c) Discuss the concerns your colleagues have and as a group work to alleviate these so everyone is comfortable before you have to attend the protest.

This is the most suitable course of action because this shows emotional awareness of your colleagues feelings and also demonstrates supportive and inspirational behaviour.

Q10. c) Confirm that you are responding to the call but ask for backup to be prepared to assist.

This is the most suitable course of action because whilst the safety of yourself and your colleague is paramount it would be negligent to not attend the reported incident.

Q11. c) Sympathise with your colleague that they are in an unfortunate position but you cannot do what they're asking. When you file the statement, alert your Sergeant to the request your colleague made.

This is the most suitable course of action because whilst you can acknowledge that this information must be difficult for your colleague to process, the behaviour they have displayed is not compatible with the values of the police.

Q12. b) Organise an event for the community which highlights the importance of accepting a variety of cultures within society and the consequences for crimes such as vandalism.

This is the most suitable course of action because you should encourage inclusivity within the community and promote diversity it's also important to address the crimes that have been committed.

Situational Judgement Questions 4

Q1. Whilst policing an event, you overhear your colleague speaking with a member of the public.

'You must be joking if you think *that* is worth my time, what a stupid question.' Your colleague walks off and the lady begins crying.

Do you:

a) Follow your colleague, ask him to tell you what happened to justify his comment.

b) Console the woman your colleague spoke to, ask her if there's anything you can help her with. Once the matter is dealt with, ask your colleague what happened.

c) Berate your colleague in front of the woman, then apologise on his behalf. Once you return to the station file a formal complaint against your colleague.

d) Insist your colleague apologises to the woman then assure her that you will personally make sure your colleague assists her with her request.

Answer ☐

Q2. You and a fellow constable have been dispatched to a fight in the town centre on a busy Saturday night. As you're approaching you receive an update that witnesses have reported seeing a knife. When you arrive one man is lying on the ground and another is sat slumped against a shop window, there are groups of people starting to gather in the area.

Do you:

a) Ask your colleague to attend to the man lying on the ground whilst you attend to the man sat against the shop window.

b) Ask the public to keep an eye on the man lying on the ground whilst you and your colleague approach the man slumped against the window, together.

c) Radio for back up, wait in the car until backup arrives and there are more of you to tackle to situation.

d) Locate the knife, then each attend to one of the men.

Answer

Q3. Whilst on a patrol in Ficshire Shopping Centre a woman runs up to you, she is crying and you manage to understand that her daughter has wondered off and she cannot find her. The lady is inconsolable and screaming.

How do you reply to the woman:

a) 'Ma'am, I am going to help you, but you must calm down first.'

b) 'Okay, I know you're scared but I'm going to radio an alert to all security staff and all stores, can you tell me what she is wearing?'

c) 'Oh no, I'll have the exits closed immediately, noone will leave the centre until we've found her!'

d) 'Where did you last see her? I'm going to do everything I can to help you find her.'

Answer

Q4. You are preparing important files to apply for a warrant to search a property. Just as you are about to submit the files, you notice the address for the property is incorrect. Rechecking all the paperwork and updating the error correctly will delay the application by several days.

Do you:

a) Correct the error yourself by writing the correct address over the incorrect one and submit the application as soon as possible.

b) Find the officer who filled in the paperwork, double-check the address with them and ask them to update the form. Take responsibility yourself for the delay.

c) Recheck the paperwork to confirm the correct address and update the form.

d) Submit the files as they are, but include a note that explains the address has been filled in incorrectly and confirm the correct address.

Q5. Ficshire is being plagued by a group of teenagers on dirt bikes who are driving on private property owned by a local farmer. Each time you have been called out, the teenagers escape via a trail you are unable to follow in your car. The residents are requesting to know what you plan to do to resolve this.

Do you:

a) Work with the local farmer to secure his property and block access from his land, to the trail.

b) Advise the residents that as this is occurring on private property the landowner is required to determine a solution.

c) Request off-road bikes for officers who patrol that area so they can follow the teenagers along the trail.

d) Ask residents to video the teenagers and submit all recordings to aid with identification of the offenders.

Answer

Q6. Ficshire Council have requested a meeting to discuss how to tackle motorists who are driving at dangerously fast speeds along Station Road. You have repeatedly suggested traffic calming measures such as speed bumps, and speed cameras. To date, Ficshire Council have not proceeded with implementing either of these measures.

Do you:

a) Refer the council to your previous suggestions, include statistics that highlight the effectiveness of traffic calming measures to reinforce your reasoning.

b) Remind the council of your previous suggestions, advise that you cannot assist further as they have not executed the solutions you've already provided.

c) Discuss the measures you have previously recommended. Ask if there are any concerns with these suggestions or if there is another approach that would be more favourable.

d) Suggest raising the speed limit for Station Road so that the motorists will not longer be breaching the speed limit.

Answer [ ]

Q7. Whilst on patrol you notice a man drop some cash from his pocket, you navigate across the busy high street to pick up the man's money and return it to him. Once you are on the other side of the street you notice a woman pick up some money from the ground and begin counting it.

Do you:

a) Catch up to the man and let him know he dropped some money which has been picked up by a woman.

b) Hang back and watch the woman to see what she does next.

c) Approach the woman and gently question her about the money.

d) Place the woman under arrest, then alert the man to what has happened.

Answer

Q8. You have just finished a patrol and are heading back to the station to end your shift. As you are walking down Ficshire High Street you notice two woman leaving a high-end cosmetics store. They don't have a shopping bag but they have set the store's anti-theft alarm off, the security guard hasn't noticed and the women don't seem to have any intention of stopping.

Do you:

a) Place both women under arrest, then alert the store's security guard to the situation so they can take over.

b) Inform the security guard what you have witnessed so he can respond to the situation accordingly.

c) Follow the women to see if they go into any other stores in the High Street, if you suspect they are shoplifting from another shop, confront them.

d) Continue heading back to the station, your shift is over and the security guard should be dealing this situations like this.

Answer

Q9. You are on your way to attend a dispute between two neighbours. As you arrive and get out of your car you hear them arguing.

Woman 1: 'The likes of you and your wife aren't welcome around here, you make me sick.'

Woman 2: 'Say one more thing like that and I'll knock you spark out!'

Woman 1: 'You're disgusting, I'm sure this Police Officer will agree...'

How do you respond:

a) Tell Woman 1 that your opinion does not matter in this dispute and advise them to be civil to one another or further action may be taken against them both.

b) Sympathise with Woman 2 and demand Woman 1 returns to her house immediately.

c) Apologise to Woman 2 for the comments she has endured and ask if she wants to press charges against Woman 1.

d) Tell Woman 1 that you will not tolerate the comments she is making, then speak with both women independently to ascertain what their argument is about.

Answer

Q10. A young girl has been stealing from her parents, after several failed attempts to correct this behaviour the parents have asked you to have a word with the girl - they do not want to pursue criminal charges against their own daughter.

What is your first step:

a) Tell the girl that although it's her parent's wish that she is not charged for stealing from them, you have a duty to enforce the law so she will need to accompany you to the station.

b) Ask the girl why she is stealing to determine the root of the problem.

c) Explain to the girl what would happen if someone did want to prosecute her for theft, describe the consequences this could have.

d) Make the girl pay her parents back for everything she stole from them.

Answer

Q11. You are on patrol when you notice a man and woman arguing loudly in the street. You approach them to find out what's wrong and learn that the woman has just found out the man, her husband, has been unfaithful to her. She is very upset and threatening to burn all of his belongings when she gets home.

Do you:

a) Ask the woman to attend the station with you where she can discuss what has happened and have time to process the infidelity and compose herself.

b) Recommend both of them continue their conversation when their emotions aren't as high and remind the woman that destruction of property in an offence.

c) Suggest the man return homes first and removes his belongings.

d) Apologise for interfering and let them carry on.

Answer

Q12. You are enjoying a relaxing weekend off when you are contacted by a colleague asking if you can cover another constable's shift as they have unexpectedly taken ill and are unable to work. The overtime would be very beneficial as your husband's salary has recently been cut, however you had a lot to drink the previous night and you are sure you are still over the limit to drive.

Do you:

a) Offer to work in a few hours when you will have less alcohol still in your system.

b) Explain that you have been drinking the night before so unfortunately you are unable to work right now.

c) Ask if your colleague can pick you up as you cannot drive due to drinking the previous night.

d) Call your Sergeant, explain that you have been drinking the night before and are not confident you are fit to drive. Ask if he deems it okay for you to cover this shift.

Answer

Situational Judgement 4 Answers

Q1. b) Console the woman your colleague spoke to, ask her if there's anything you can help her with. Once the matter is dealt with, ask your colleague what happened.

This is the most suitable course of action because your first response should be to check the well-being of the woman who is upset and see if you are able to assist her. Once this is resolved, you should speak to your colleague about his reaction.

Q2. d) Locate the knife, then each attend to one of the men.

This is the most suitable course of action because in a situation where there is a suspected weapon you must first locate and secure this to ensure yourself, your colleague/s and general public are safe and noone else can be injured.

Q3. b) 'Okay, I know you're scared but I'm going to radio an alert to all security staff and all stores, can you tell me what she is wearing?'

This is the most suitable course of action because you are showing empathy to the woman whilst also taking control of the situation and taking immediate action.

Q4. b) Find the officer who filled in the paperwork, double-check the address with them and ask them to update the form. Take responsibility yourself for the delay.

This is the most suitable course of action because submitting the documents accurately is always a top priority. It's also important that although the typo on the form was not yours, you are showing an ability to take ownership of the situation.

Q5. a) Work with the local farmer to secure his property and block access from his land, to the trail.

This is the most suitable course of action because this shows an ability to work collaboratively with the land owner and also provides a situation which will leave the land owner and the local residents feeling that the issue is resolved.

Q6. c) Discuss the measures you have previously recommended. Ask if there are any concerns with these suggestions or if there is another approach that would be more favourable.

This is the most suitable course of action because the council are still seeking your assistance so a resolution must be found and by approaching your previous suggestions in a new manner may help you determine why they have not be implemented before.

Q7. c) Approach the woman and gently question her about the money.

This is the most suitable course of action because whilst the two incidents may be a coincidence it is important to be proactive and follow up with the woman. It would be reckless to jump to any conclusions without speaking to the women first.

Q8. b) Inform the security guard what you have witnessed so he can respond to the situation accordingly.

This is the most suitable course of action because the security guard must be alerted that the store's alarm has been activated so they can check why the women have set the alarm off.

Police Officer Online Assessment Tests   97

Q9. d) Tell Woman 1 that you will not tolerate the comments she is making, then speak with both women independently to ascertain what their argument is about.

This is the most suitable course of action because you must be clear that the comments made by Woman 1 are unacceptable and will not be tolerated. Then, by speaking to both women separately, you will be able to gain a better understanding of the dispute from both women's point of view.

Q10. b) Ask the girl why she is stealing to determine the root of the problem.

This is the most suitable course of action because the girl's parents have specifically requested that you speak to their daughter, and not issue a punishment. By speaking with her, you may be able to identify if anything has happened to trigger this behaviour. Once this has been identified, it will be easier to resolve the issue.

Q11. b) Recommend both of them continue their conversation when their emotions aren't as high and remind the woman that destruction of property in an offence.

This is the most suitable course of action because although the circumstances are understandably fraught with emotion you must address the comment you have heard regarding destruction of property. This is also a situation that, currently, does not require your input.

Q12. b) Explain that you have been drinking the night before so unfortunately you are unable to work right now.

This is the most suitable course of action because with any alcohol remaining in your system, you are not fit to work.

Written Exercises

Written Exercise 1

To: PC Jones

From: Sergeant Smith

Date: 04.12.2019

We have received a number of complaints from shop owners regarding people attempting to steal food items and harassing customers in and outside the shops. Shop owners are stating that they are losing trade because of this and are demanding action from the police.

Can you please look into this issue and report back with your recommendations to reduce the crime on the high street and advise why we are seeing an increase in the offences and also advise on the below.

1. What are the main issues raised and how are these issues impacting the community?
2. Provide your recommendations on how we can resolve these issues.
3. How will these recommendations have a positive impact on the community?
4. Are there any potential risks to the community?
5. What can be done to provide reassurance for the community?

Many thanks

Sergeant Smith

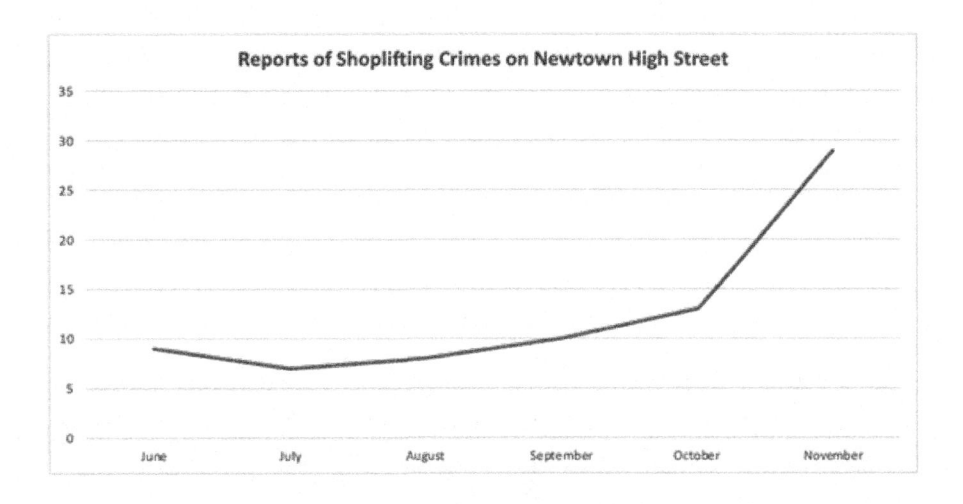

Attachment 1: Chart of reported crimes in the high street.

Reports of Shoplifting Crimes on Newtown High Street

Line chart showing reported shoplifting crimes from June to November. Values approximately: June 9, July 7, August 8, September 10, October 13, November 29.

Attachment 2: Eyewitness statements and complaint call from local resident

Eyewitness statement 1

A local shop keeper has stated that he had seen a well-known shop lifter in the area known as 'Tea-Leaf Trevor' hanging around the high street, dressed smartly in his signature attire. However, he also stated that he had not witnessed him stealing anything. (Tea-Leaf Trevor was released from prison at the end of September after serving five years for stealing high priced items from electrical stores).

Eyewitness statement 2

The owner of the local mini-market chased a homeless man out of his shop after he caught him stealing a bag of apples and some protein bars. The shop keeper stated that he did not recognise the person but said that it looked like they had been sleeping rough and his clothes were very dirty.

Complaint call

A local resident Gary Edwards has called the station and expressed concerns regarding harassment from a number of homeless people in the high street. Mr Edwards stated, on the 7th November when he was out shopping, he was stopped and harassed by a number of people begging him for money. He said this had also happened the previous week.

Attachment 3: Map of High Street showing affected shops

Gary's Games Shop lifting incidents: 2 in July, 1 in August, 2 in September	**Currently Vacant** Last Occupied by Homeless Food hub and shelter closed from Middle of October. Shelter Re-opened in Station Road
Martins Greengrocer Shop lifting incidents: 7 in November	**Pharmacy** Shop lifting incidents: 2 in June, 1 in August
Sky Right Clothes Department Store Shop lifting incidents: 1 in June, 2 in August	**Food for Thought Food Supermarket** Shop lifting incidents: 2 in September, 6 in October, 6 in November
Booths Electrical Store Shop lifting incidents: 0	
Magnum Furniture Shop lifting incidents: 3 in June	**Victory Music** Shop lifting incidents: 1 in June, 3 in September
Windy Pet Store Shop lifting incidents: 1 in June, 1 in July, 1 September	**Timber Builders and Supplies** Shop lifting incidents: 1 in November
Currently Vacant Last Occupied by High street Cafe Closed from August 0 incidents	**Maces Newsagent** Shop lifting incidents: 3 in July, 2 in August, 1 in September
	Blakey's Shoes Shop lifting incidents: 2 in July, 3 in August, 1 in September
Jacksons Foodmarkets Shop lifting incidents: 3 in October, 9 in November	**Corner Food Supplies** Shop lifting incidents: 1 in June, 5 in October, 6 in November

Flow of traffic

YOUR ANSWER / NOTES

Written Exercise 1 Answers

Suggested points for your answer:

1. What are the main issues raised and how are these affecting the community?

- There are a number of thefts from shops and members of the community being harassed by people begging for money.
- The shop keepers are concerned that the thefts are impacting their profits and will prevent customers shopping in their stores.
- The community will start to avoid the high street if they continue to be harassed.
- This will have a negative impact upon the town as the drop in sales could cause shops to close.

2. Provide your recommendations on how we can resolve these issues.

- We need to be analytical in our approach to ascertain the cause.
- But first, to prevent further occurrences, you should consider having extra patrols along the high street. This will achieve a number of things; provide reassurance to the community, gather information from the community, and provide advice. A physical presence will also deter offenders and present the opportunity to witness offences in progress and act accordingly.
- You can see from the graph that there is a gradual rise between July and October, but then a sharp rise between October and November. So, the catalyst for the issue most likely occurred in October.
- You could speak to 'Tea-Leaf Trevor', although from the witness statements, he does not fit the crime profile. Trevor is not known for stealing food, and dresses smartly in suits.

- Looking at the map of the impacted high street stores, the shops most affected are food stores and the majority of incidents are in October/November.

- The map of the high street highlights the number of vacant shops. One of them is a homeless shelter/ food hub which was closed from October and re-opened in Station Road.

- It's possible because of the closure, members of the homeless community are stealing food as they have lost their supply of food. They may be unaware of the reopened shelter/hub in Station Road. One of the shopkeepers stated that he had chased a homeless man out of his shop after catching him stealing food items and another person stated he was harassed by a homeless man on the high street.

- You should speak to members of the homeless community to inform them of the reopened shelter in Station Road and provide details of the location. As it seems likely, from the information given, that a number of homeless people are responsible for the thefts and harassment. You need to make it clear that if anyone is caught stealing or harassing other members of the community further action will be taken.

- Remember that the homeless people are still members of the community and you should offer your assistance as and when required. All members of the community need to be treated with equal respect and integrity.

3. How will these recommendations have a positive impact on the community?

- The extra patrols will give the wider community confidence that the matter is being addressed, and will help the shoppers to feel safer walking down the high street.

- This will also help to prevent further incidents of shoplifting.

- By directing the homeless community towards the new hub and shelter they can utilise the facilities available so they can get food and a safe place to sleep.

4. Are there any risks to the community?

- The increased presence of the police in the high street could push offenders to other areas further afield.
- The increased presence could also scare shoppers away from the high street, as they may feel uneasy with the extra police patrols.
- Directing the homeless community to the shelter in Station Road, could cause strain on this shelter, as it could become overwhelmed with the extra people using their services.

5. What can be done to provide reassurance to the community?

- The extra patrols should speak to the members of the community on the high street to tell them what action the police are taking and ask if there is anything they need assistance with.
- Speak to the shopkeepers to advise them of the extra patrols and provide an immediate point of contact so the patrols can respond quickly as soon as an incident is reported.
- Add signage illustrating the increased patrols to act as a deterrent to any potential shoplifters and the action that will be taken with any individuals caught.
- You could also arrange a meeting with the local shopkeepers to advise on the actions you are taking and offer advice on how they can protect their stores from shoplifting by installing CCTV and other security measures.

Written Exercise 2

Email from Sergeant:

Date: 16.10.2018

We have received a complaint from Mr Alan Jones, who has stated his car has been damaged, whilst parked on a residential street after attending a football match at Newtown Utd's stadium.

Mr Jones stated that when he was returning to his vehicle after the match, he witnessed one of the residents damage his car by running a key down the side of it. Mr Jones then saw the person in question enter a house on the same road (Vincent Square) which was adjacent to the parked vehicle. Mr Jones, then knocked on the door to confront the person about the damage to the vehicle, and was told the following. 'I am fed up with people parking outside my house on matchdays' and slammed the door shut.

We have contacted the person accused of the damage and they have been charged with a public order offence, and the person in question has offered to pay for repairs to the vehicle.

After looking more closely into this, it seems we have had a number of complaints from local residents regarding supporters parking outside residents' houses on matchdays. Can you please look into this issue and propose a resolution which suits both the residents and supporters visiting on matchday? To assist you with this task, I have attached a number of supporting documents.

1. What are the main issues raised and how are these issues impacting the community?
2. Provide your recommendations on how we can resolve these issues.
3. How will these recommendations have a positive impact on the community?
4. Are there any potential risks to the community?
5. What can be done to provide reassurance for the community?

Attachment 1: Map of area with public car park information and parking permit regulations for Vincent Square

> Residents Parking between the hours of 8am – 2pm Monday to Saturday
>
> Residents only parking on matchdays from 2pm

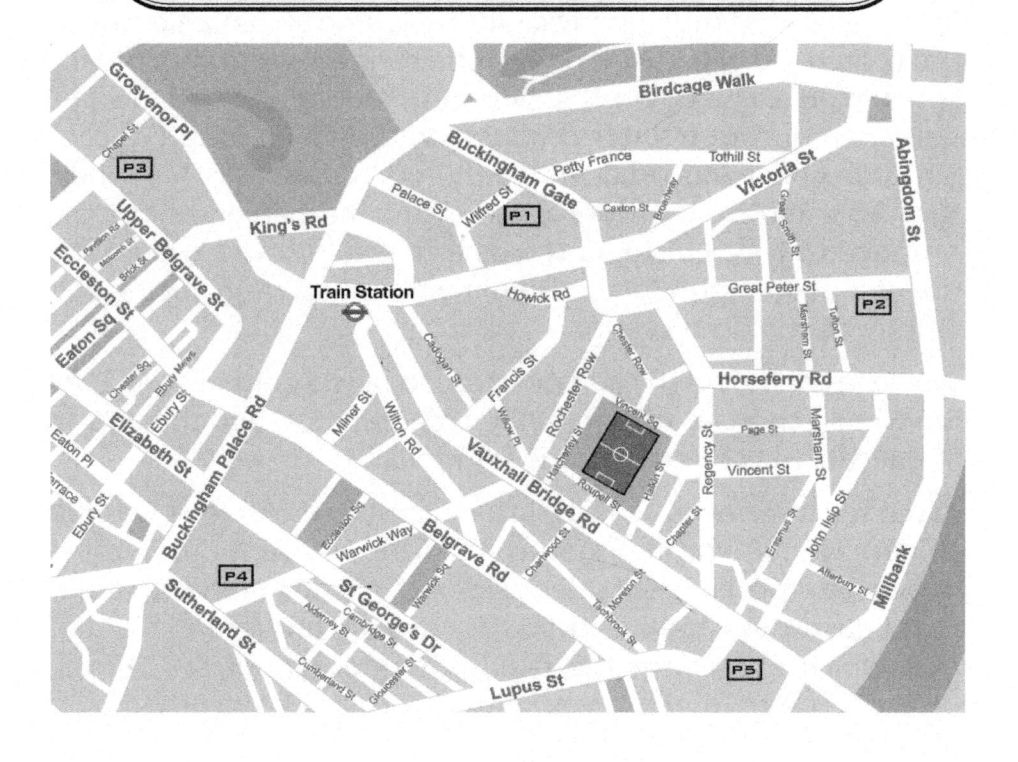

Car Park location	Distance from Ground	Spaces	Average capacity of filled spaces during matches
Chapel Street (P3)	1.2 km	859	85%
Wilfred Street (P1)	700 m	245	41%
Lupus Street (P5)	328 m	900	91% (matchdays)
Sutherland Street (P4)	1.1 km	600	22%
Tufton Street (P2)	450 m	750	63%

It is also worth noting the local train station is 1.3 km from the ground

Attachment 2: Fixture List

Date	Opponent	Home/Away
Sat 27th Oct 15:00	Littletown City	Home
Tue 30th Oct 19:45	Inglebrook Town	Home
Sat 3rd Nov 17:30	Newbury FC	Away
Sat 10th Nov 15:00	Richampton	Home
Wed 14th Nov 20:00	Eastborough Utd	Away
Tue 20th Nov 20:00	Forest Hill Rovers	Home
Sat 24th Nov 13:30	Poolchester	Home

Attachment 3: Letter from Chairman of Newtown Utd to supporters from matchday program

Dear Supporter,

As an incentive to get the local community through the turnstiles and to reduce the traffic around the local area on matchdays, we have negotiated a deal with the local rail company to offer reduced rail fares to our supporters on matchdays. To take advantage of this offer, all you need to do is produce your e-ticket when purchasing your rail ticket and you will receive 25% off the fare. This offer is only available to home supporters from the local area.

We have also partnered with the local council for reduced rate parking and free shuttle bus transfer to the ground on matchdays, but this must be booked in advance at least 24 hours prior to matchday. For more information and booking please visit our website.

We are also delighted to announce that we will be continuing our free parking inside the stadium car park for our season ticket holders and supporters who are valid disabled blue badge holders.

I would also like to remind supporters that the residential streets around the four sides of the ground are for resident permit holders use only on matchdays and NOT just between the hours of 8:00am and 2:00pm, as is the case on non-matchdays.

Thank you for your continued support and up the Town!

Yours sincerely

Johnson Cartwright

Chairman

YOUR ANSWER / NOTES

Written Exercise 2 Answers

Suggested answer could include the following:

1. What are the main issues the community are facing?

- The local community are facing issues with parking during matchdays around the ground in permit-only areas.
- This is also causing congestion issues and having a negative impact on the environment, with the excess traffic on matchdays.
- This has also caused an issue where a resident has vandalised a supporter's vehicle.
- This is causing tension between the residents and the visiting supporters.

2. Provide your recommendations on how we can resolve these issues?

- There are two core issues that need addressing here; to prevent supporters parking around the permit areas of the ground and also to accommodate the supporters travelling to the ground on matchdays.
- The permit parking on matchdays only starts from 2pm. We should work collaboratively with the council to change this so the areas around the ground are permit only for the entire day until the match has finished.
- Collaborate further with the council to put signage around the town with directions to the town's car parks.
- Advise the club to publish the deals they have available not only in their programme but also in the local press and radio.
- Also advise the club to announce information regarding the parking restrictions and also the park and ride, and reduced rail fare offers before kick-off and at half time over the stadium announcement system.

- Increase patrols around the permit parking areas to prevent unauthorised vehicles parking on match days.
- Ensure the vandalism to the vehicle is dealt with as equal to the wider issues faced. Although this is an isolated incident this has to be enforced.

3. How will these recommendations have a positive impact on the community?
- The actions taken will help to resolve the issues for both the residents and the visiting supporters.
- Increased patrols will help to promote a positive image of the police to the residents that the matter is being dealt with seriously and will also be a deterrent for any supporters still attempting to park their vehicles in the permit only roads around the stadium.
- By partnering with the club and the council, you are showing a collaborative proactive approach to deal with the issue from the perspective of supporters and residents.
- By enforcing the law for the criminal damage to the vehicle this will provide confidence that this matter is being dealt with, although the vehicle was parked illegally.

4. Are there any potential risks to the community?
- Although the increased presence of the police will be of comfort to some, this may not be the case for all, as some of the community will be uneasy with the increased police presence.
- There is a risk that changing the permit rules around the stadium could result in supporters parking illegally in other areas of the town. Not only could this be a drain on resources, but could potentially raise tensions in these areas. You need to be mindful of the issues the actions could cause other residents who are not currently affected.
- The influx of vehicles directed to other car parks could cause potential issues for other users of the car park not

being able to park on match days. The same could be said for rail passengers, as carriages may be more congested with an influx of football supporters.

5. What can be done to provide reassurance for the community?
- In your answer you must show impartiality to ensure that both the residents/supporters are given the same service equally.
- In your answer you should communicate with the community what actions you have taken and that you will continue to monitor the situation to ensure the current actions are effective.
- In your answer also communicate with any of the wider community to explain the reasoning behind the actions and ask for their feedback on how the actions are affecting them.

Written Exercise 3

To: PC Jones

From: Sergeant Smith

Date: 11.07.2020

Hello PC Jones,

We have received a complaint from a gentleman who works for a door-to-door sales company. The gentleman in question, Mark Atherton, said he was threatened by a homeowner who became angry and abusive after he knocked on their door to tell them about a new range of products on offer.

According to Mr Atherton, as soon as the occupant answered the door, they were verbally abusive and even attempted to grab Mr Atherton and push him onto the ground. According to his statement, Mr Atherton managed to move out of the way to prevent himself stumbling. He also added he was very surprised by the homeowner's reaction as the household in question had purchased items on more than one occasion in the past few months.

Mr Atherton is happy not to press charges as no harm was done, but we have spoken to the homeowner in question for his version of the events. You will find this attached as well as other documents to assist you.

1. What are the main issues raised and how are these issues impacting the community?
2. Provide your recommendations on how we can resolve these issues.
3. How will these recommendations have a positive impact on the community?
4. Are there any potential risks to the community?
5. What can be done to provide reassurance for the community?

Many thanks

Sergeant Smith

Attachment 1: Statement from homeowner

These people are a menace, they always seem to come when I am not in! Unfortunately, my wife normally answers and ends up buying some of their nonsense. According to my wife the tactics are quite intimidating and definitely not that of a friendly salesman. On three occasions she has been forced to purchase items through their aggressive tactics. Once we ended up with dishwasher tablets. We do not even have a dishwasher! A number of our neighbours have also complained to trading standards and asked the council to prevent any door-to-door salesmen selling on our street.

Attachment 2: Complaint to council from resident regarding door-to-door selling

Dear Sir/Madam,

I am writing to you to complain about the number of cold-calling salesmen we have had knocking on our door and our neighbour's doors. We live in Stone Acre Crossing which is situated in the town of Lionhare.

For the last three months we have been bombarded on a daily basis by salesmen from a company called Homeware International. They are extremely pushy and aggressive with their sales tactics. On one occasion they tried to prevent me closing my door when I told them I was not interested.

After this, which was the final straw, I tried to contact someone in their head office, but after numerous attempts without success I feel that I have to contact the authorities as this intimidating behaviour needs to stop.

This behaviour is unacceptable and myself and my neighbours are becoming afraid to answer our front doors.

This is not the first time myself or my neighbours have complained to the council regarding this, but as of yet we have seen no action. Can you please advise what you can do about this issue before this escalates further?

Yours sincerely

Eric Morris, Stone Acre resident.

Attachment 3: Reply to Mr Morris from Lionhare council

Dear Mr Morris,

Thank you for your letter and letting us know of the problems you are experiencing.

We have contacted the company and have sent an official letter to ask them to explain their sales tactics and policy and to cease with their sales operation in the area.

With sales companies of this nature the council has strict policies which all companies who are based in and operating in the area have to comply with. However, the company in question is not based in Lionhare so does not fall under the local policy. Please note, this does not mean we are not able to take action. What we can do is this:

Each resident can apply for a cold calling exemption notice which you display on your front door or window, so this is visible for all potential cold-calling salesmen to see. Once displayed, any company wishing to offer products via door-to-door sales has to seek written permission from the resident before proceeding. If you do not respond giving permission in writing then the company in question will be unable to offer their services or products.

To get your exemption notice, please apply for this via the resident services at www.lionharecouncil.gov.uk

Once your application has been received, please allow 30 days for your exemption notice display sticker to arrive.

If you have any further queries, or need any further help please let me know.

Many thanks,

Emily Davies

Lionhare Council

Attachment 4: Customer reviews of Homeware International

1-star review from John W, Lionhare

This company's sales tactics are pushy and aggressive! When I said I was not interested, he started shouting at me!

1-star review from David Renshaw, Lionhare

I have one of their sales reps at my front door at least once a week. Each time I have told them that I am not interested in what they have to offer, but they keep returning week after week. This is now bordering on harassment.

2-star review from Ian H, Lionhare.

Purchased some shoe polish from this company which said it was black. When I tried to use it the colour of the polish was brown! They exchanged the polish the following week when they visited again – which they seem to every week! Overall, I am not satisfied with the service and will not use them again. Also, the company's sales tactics are aggressive and pushy. This seems to be a company mandate as I have had visits from various different reps and all have had the same aggressive approach.

5-star review from Lucy Johnson, Lionhare

Purchased some tea towels and ironing board cover from Homeware International and would have to say that the quality of product and level of service has been excellent. Far more cost effective than similar products I have bought from the high street before. Highly recommended.

YOUR ANSWER / NOTES

Written Exercise 3 Answers

Suggested answer could include the following:

1. What are the main issues the community are facing?

- A local salesman was nearly assaulted by an angry homeowner when he knocked on the door to offer his latest products.
- Some residents of Stone Acre Crossing feel they are being harassed by salesmen from a door-to-door sales company.
- A number of complaints suggest that members of the community are intimidated by the sales company's tactics and now feel frightened to open their front doors.
- The local community seem also frustrated by the lack of action by the local council.

2. Provide your recommendations on how we can resolve these issues?

- There are number of issues that need to be resolved here. One is the attempted assault. Although the resident was frustrated and angry, which is understandable, his actions were unacceptable. The residents must be warned that any reports regarding this type of conduct will be followed up and action will be taken accordingly.
- You should take ownership of the situation and make contact with the company in question regarding the tactics of the sales personnel. Advise that they should cease with these pushy sales tactics immediately, otherwise face further action.
- Arrange patrols for Stone Acre Crossing to aid the residents and be able to quickly respond to any further incidents.
- You should collaborate with the council to find a working solution for all residents. Looking at the reviews, it would seem that not all residents are unhappy with the service. With this in mind you could arrange with the council to

post cold calling exemption notices, with instructions, to all residents. The resident can then decide whether or not they want to display the notice at their front door.

- The notice should also include a contact number for any queries regarding the exemption notice and to report any breaches to.
- Arrange with the council to follow up with any residents issued with the notices to assist with any further unwelcome calls.
- Collaborate with the council to construct a more robust policy regarding cold-calling companies.

3. How will these recommendations have a positive impact on the community?
- By arranging the patrols, you are taking a proactive step to monitor the situation and will be able to respond in a timely manner to any incidents.
- By contacting the company, you are giving them the opportunity to investigate the issue themselves and take action internally. It may be they are unaware of the actions of the sales personnel and may be able to prevent further occurrences themselves.
- Working with the council to provide a solution shows collaboration. Not all residents are unhappy with the service of the company, so by issuing the exemption notices to the residents they can choose whether they want to display the notice. This is more efficient then a full ban, as this could leave some of the community unhappy.
- By working with council and following up with the community you are not only showing support to the residents but this also allows you to analyse whether any further action is required.
- By dealing with the initial attempted assault, you are showing impartiality by warning the residents of the consequences of any such actions.

4. Are there any potential risks to the community?

- It is possible that the increased patrols will have a negative effect on some of the community, who may see this as unwelcome.

- The company may decide to move to another area, which could have a negative impact on that community and would also disappoint some of the residents in Stone Acre Crossing who are happy with the services provided.

5. What can be done to provide reassurance for the community?

- Hold a joint meeting with the council and residents to explain what is being done to address the concerns within the community.

- Advise the residents that the company in question has been officially contacted and warned about their current conduct and the consequences if they do not comply with exemption notices which have been issued and displayed by residents.

- Explain that the patrols are there specifically to monitor and deal with any further incidents. Remind the residents of the contact number on the exemption notice, which can be used to contact the police/council if they encounter any issues.

- Set up a neighbourhood support group. This will help residents feel they are part of the resolution and provides an excellent basis for reporting any incidents.

Written Exercise 4

To: PC Jones

From: Sergeant Smith

Subject: Multiple thefts from garages blocks in the housing estate of Westbank Estate, Ficshire

Hi PC Jones,

We have received a number of reports of break-ins to resident's garages in Westbank Estate, Ficshire.

As you know Westbank Estate is one of the UK's largest housing estates and covers quite a large area within a radius of four miles. So far, we have no suspects and very minimal leads. What we do know is that the thieves are targeting certain items such as power tools, and other high-end electrical equipment and this is only happening in areas where there is no CCTV. So far, the crimes have been reported in two locations; Marden Close and Davies Road on Westbank Estate, both at opposite ends of the estate to each other. There has been a total of ten incidents in the last two weeks. The local residents are becoming frustrated with the lack of progress and some residents are threatening to take the law into their own hands.

Please look into these issues and advise your recommendations on how we can catch those responsible but also help on how to secure the resident's property? Please see attached documents which I have received which will assist you.

1. What are the main issues raised and how are these issues impacting the community?
2. Provide your recommendations on how we can resolve these issues.
3. How will these recommendations have a positive impact on the community?
4. Are there any potential risks to the community?
5. What can be done to provide reassurance for the community?

Attachment 1: Map of Davies Road. Burgled garages have been highlighted.

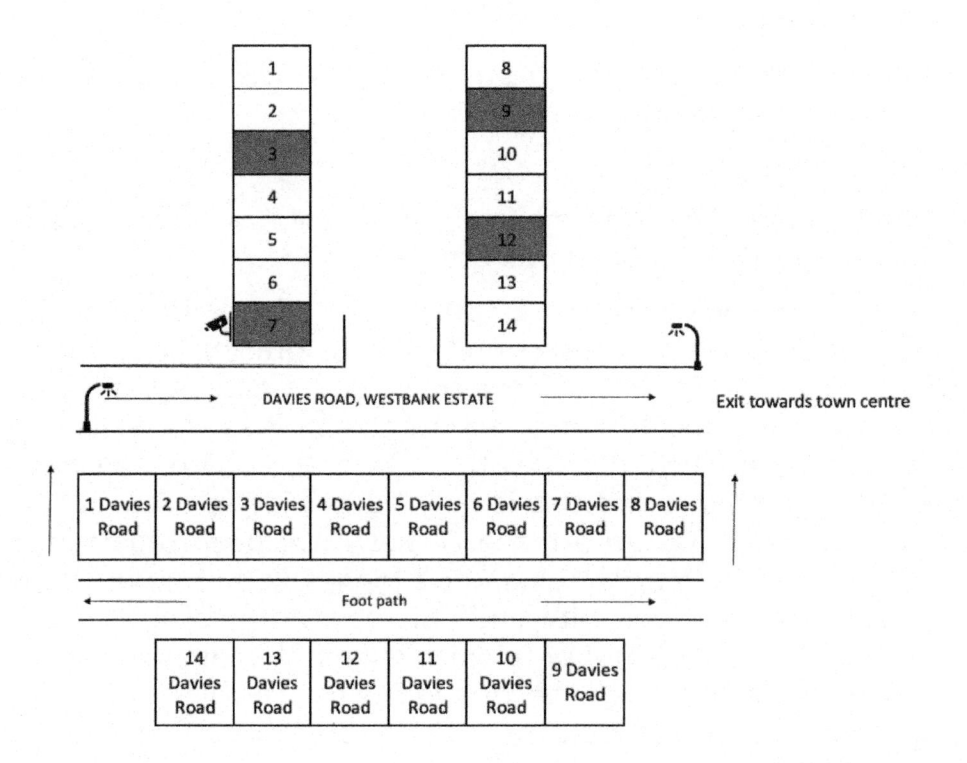

	1			8	
	2			9	
	3			10	
	4			11	
	5			12	
	6			13	
	7			14	

DAVIES ROAD, WESTBANK ESTATE → Exit towards town centre

1 Davies Road	2 Davies Road	3 Davies Road	4 Davies Road	5 Davies Road	6 Davies Road	7 Davies Road	8 Davies Road

← Foot path →

14 Davies Road	13 Davies Road	12 Davies Road	11 Davies Road	10 Davies Road	9 Davies Road

Attachment 2: Map of Marden Close. Burgled garages have been highlighted.

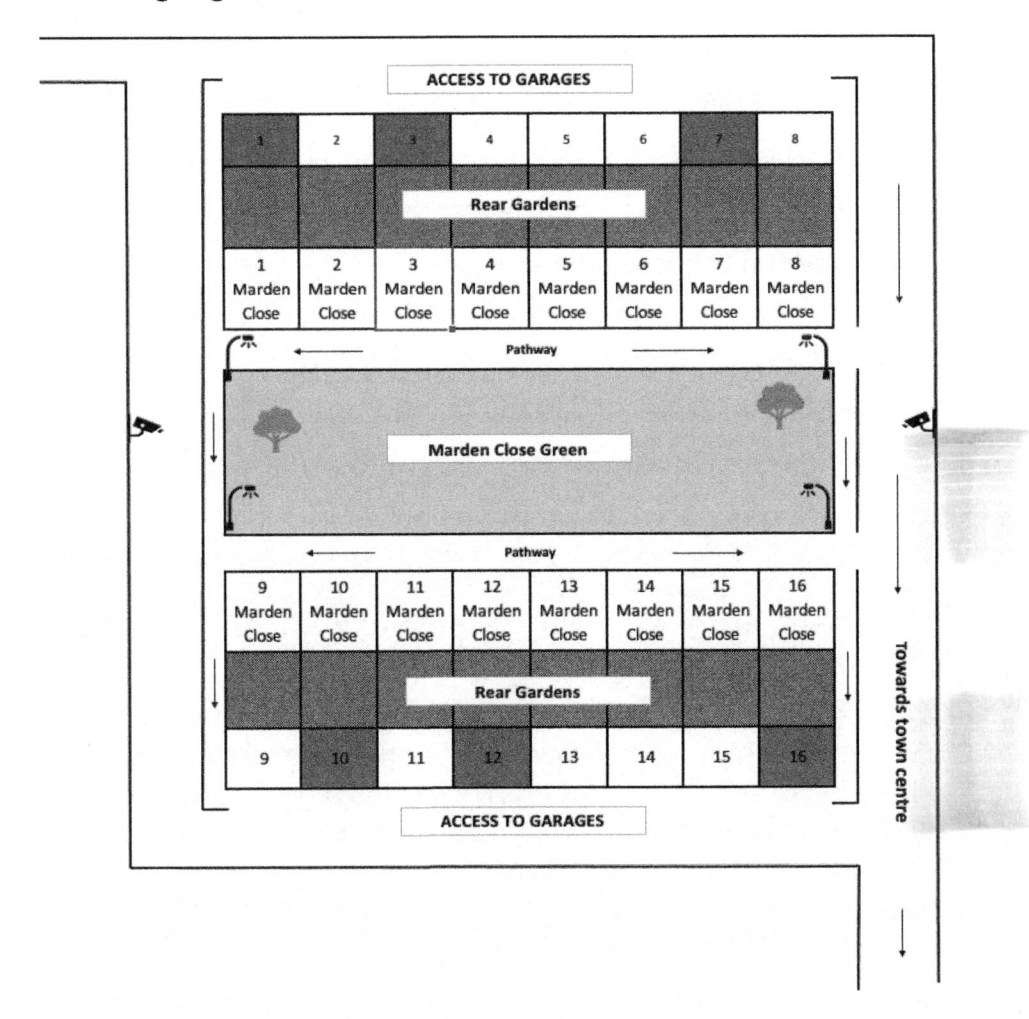

Attachment 3: List of items taken from garages

* 3 Davies Road; Petrol lawnmower and chainsaw.
* 7 Davies Road; Circular saw, tool box and hammer drill.
* 9 Davies Road; No items taken.
* 12 Davies Road; Electric strimmer and hedge trimmer.
* 1 Marden Close; Concrete mixer and electric screwdriver.
* 3 Marden Close; Electric mower.
* 7 Marden Close; Toolbox and numerous power tools including a sander, drill and circular saw.
* 10 Marden Close; No items taken.
* 12 Marden Close; Car jack, lawn-mower and toolbox.
* 16 Marden Close; No items taken.

Attachment 4: Eyewitness statement from resident of 14 Marden Close.

I was returning from taking my dog for a walk in the woods close to the town centre when I saw three men acting suspiciously just to the side of our garage block. There was a grey van parked on the corner of the road next to the garages. Unfortunately, I didn't notice the registration as it was dark and my eyesight is not the best these days! However, as I approached, they rushed into the van and drove off, which of course raised my suspicions.

I decided to walk round to the garages to check and I could see that numbers 16, 12 and 10's garage doors had been forced open. Outside the garage of number 16 I could see a few items stacked near the garage door. It looked like a skill saw and tool box which I thought was odd. I could not see any items outside either number 10 or 12. I then called the police and told my neighbours of the forced entry to their garages.

YOUR ANSWER / NOTES

Written Exercise 4 Answers

Suggested answer could include the following:

1. What are the main issues raised and how are these impacting the community?

- A number of residents have had their garages burgled or broken into.
- This is causing concerns around the entire estate as the residents are concerned that their properties could be next.
- The residents are also becoming increasingly frustrated by the lack of progress in catching the person/s responsible and this is causing tension between the police and the local community.
- Members of the community, are also threatening to take matters into their own hands if the lack of progress continues.

2. Provide your recommendations on how we can resolve these issues?

- You could suggest that extra patrols should be deployed on the estate to act as a deterrent and to offer support and advice to the community. This could also help to catch those responsible. Patrols need to be visible 24 hours per day.
- Be vigilant and check garage areas twice as often than areas which are covered by CCTV.
- You could collaborate with the local council to advise residents on the estate to be more vigilant and install extra security devices to their properties if possible.
- Analyse the CCTV camera data on the side of the road adjacent to Marden Close Green as this may have picked up the grey van on camera.
- Seek to obtain a contract with a security company who would provide a discount if a set amount of neighbours utilised their services.

- Check the vehicle database for any local people who own a grey van and arrange to speak to any persons of interest. Canvass the local community to see if they know of anyone locally with a grey van.

- The list of stolen items mainly consists of power tools and gardening equipment such as lawn mowers and strimmers. It's possible that the criminals are selling this equipment via online auction sites/local markets, so you could cross reference the stolen items with newly available items online with matching descriptions.

- Collaborate with the council to get CCTV and additional lighting installed in the garage areas as a matter of urgency. You will see from the maps there is no CCTV or lighting in the garage areas.

- Tackle the issue of members of the community wanting to take matters into their own hands by working with the residents to create a neighbourhood watch group. The members of the community can then report anything suspicious directly to you, which will help them to feel empowered as they can become part of the solution. However, you must stress that any violence or unlawful behaviour towards anyone would be dealt with as per the law.

3. How will these recommendations have a positive impact on the community?

- The extra patrols in the area will provide confidence that the police are being proactive in deterring any further break-ins whilst continuing to search for the offenders.

- Working with the council to offer advice and support, plus installing CCTV and extra lighting will reassure to the residents that their garages will be safer from further occurrences.

- Including the community and creating the neighbourhood watch group will help ease the tensions between the police and residents as you are involving them in the solution. This will also provide an efficient way for the residents to report any suspicious activity.

4. Are there any risks to the community?

- With the increased patrols, CCTV, and lighting, the thieves may relocate to another area.

- The neighbourhood watch could result in the wrong people being identified and may encourage vigilante behaviour.

- Asking the community if they are aware of anyone with the same type of van could be a potential issue for innocent residents who happen to have a grey van and may be accused of perpetrating the crimes.

- Some members of the community, not effected by the current issues, may feel uncomfortable with the level of police presence in the estate. The increased police presence may give the estate a bad reputation.

5. What can be done to provide reassurance for the community?

- Hold a joint meeting with the council, so the residents can put forward their concerns and ask any questions.

- Issue all residents with advice and support on how they can further protect their property from thieves. You should also provide a point of contact to report incidents which will ensure patrols are contacted to quickly respond.

- Reassure any members of the public who are concerned with the level of police presence in the area. Advise them of the issues at hand and that you will do your utmost to be as discreet as possible. Once the threat has been eliminated you can evaluate reducing the patrols.

Written Exercise 5

To: PC Jones

From: Sergeant Smith

Date: 19.09.2020

Hello PC Jones,

We have received a number of complaints from the residents of South Town, Lionhare, regarding noise; specifically shouting and hymn singing from the local church late into the evening. Also, the residents have stated that rubbish left by the churchgoers is strewn across the street when they leave after the service finishes at 10pm.

This is a regular occurrence as the churchgoers congregate on Tuesday evenings from 7pm until 10pm each week. We have also been contacted by the head of the church. At the church meeting last week, the service was interrupted by an angry local resident who threatened to burn the church down if they did not keep the noise down.

Can you please look into this and provide your ideas on how to resolve this issue amicably for both parties, before the situation escalates any further. I have attached some documents to this email which will assist you to answer the queries below.

1. What are the main issues raised and how are these issues impacting the community?
2. Provide your recommendations on how we can resolve these issues.
3. How will these recommendations have a positive impact on the community?
4. Are there any potential risks to the community?
5. What can be done to provide reassurance for the community?

Attachment 1: Email chain between a South Town resident and the local council.

Dear Sir/Madam,

I am writing to you today to complain about the excessive noise made by members of the local church each week on a Tuesday evening. There is excessive shouting and singing right up to 10 pm in the evening on a Tuesday night, every week! I am a shift worker who has to start work early in the morning and this level of noise is keeping me awake.

To add insult to injury, the noise they all make when leaving the church is also inconsiderate. As the weeks go on, the number of churchgoers seems to be increasing and with this, the amount of vehicles parking along the road is also growing week by week. This is causing problems for residents trying to park our cars as most of the time the spaces outside of the houses are taken by the church goers, who do not even live in South Town!

Something needs to be done about this immediately!

I await your reply,

Cecelia Dawson

> **Reply from Lionhare Council compliance officer**
>
> Dear Cecelia,
>
> Thank you for your email.
>
> We do have strict noise compliance rules in all areas of Lionhare, though this is only enforceable after 11pm.
>
> However, if you feel that the level of noise is impacting your quality of life, ie; you are unable to watch the television without disturbance, or the level of noise is keeping you awake at night, we would ask you to download a noise diary and fill this in for the next 30 days.
>
> Once this is complete and returned, we can ascertain if further action is required. If we deem so, we will contact the responsible party and ask them politely to consider any noise pollution which is affecting their neighbours. However, as this is prior to 11pm we are restricted in the action we can take.

I am very sorry that I am unable to offer any solid resolution at this time. If you do find that the noise does continue after 11pm we will be able to take enforceable action against the property in question.

Yours Sincerely,

Iain Baxter

Compliance Officer, Lionhare Council

Attachment 2: Transcript of a call to the police from Reverend Winslow Gordon from The Free Community & Gospel Church, South Town, Lionhare. 17.09.2020 at 21:40.

My name is Reverend Winslow Gordon from The Free Church in South Town, Lionhare. Yesterday I was in the middle of my closing sermon, when a man forced open our church doors and entered the building screaming 'Shut up with all your shouting and singing! If this carries on, you won't have a church to go to as I will burn the building down!' I did not recognise the man but one of our congregation, who lives near-by, knows him as a local resident, Derek Newman, who lives opposite the church.

Can someone speak to this man? We are a friendly and peaceful church community and this behaviour is unacceptable.

Attachment 3: Email from a local resident to the council regarding rubbish from the church in the street.

Hi there,

Every week, on a Wednesday morning I am awoken to rubbish and food waste strewn all over the road and pavements. This seems to be coming from the church. They leave their rubbish bags out overnight on a Tuesday evening and animals are ripping open the bags and the rubbish ends up everywhere! This is an issue as the refuse collectors do not come until Thursdays.

Not only is this an eyesore, this also presents a health risk of rats rummaging around the streets. Can you please make contact with the church about this issue? I am fed up with clearing up their rubbish every Wednesday morning.

As residents of South Street, we are growing tired with the antics of this church. Not only do we have to clear up after them, but the amount of noise on a Tuesday night is ridiculous. We have all had enough, and something needs to be done.

Please do something now!

Regards, Polly Lawrence

[Auto-response from council]

Dear Polly,

Thank you for your message.

PLEASE NOTE THIS AN AUTOMATED MESSAGE – DO NOT REPLY TO THIS EMAIL

We have received your message and will look into this and get back to you. Please note we are currently experiencing high levels of queries, and we will get back to you within 14 days.

If your query is urgent please call the council helpline on 0842 434500. Lines are open from 0800 - 1600 Monday to Friday.

Many thanks,

Lionhare Council.

Attachment 4: Harassment incident report from a resident of South Town to the police 18.09.2020

I was walking back home from work this evening and as I got close to my house, I was confronted by a number of teenagers. I recognised the children as those of my neighbours, but I am not sure which exactly which neighbours. They started hurling abuse at me and then started to throw rubbish at me and threatened that if us 'God squad' don't move on we'll get it worse next time.

I can only imagine this is a hatred attack due to me being part of the congregation of the local Free Church in South Town. This is totally wrong and these yobs need bringing to justice. I should not be victimised because of my beliefs.

YOUR ANSWER / NOTES

Written Exercise 5 Answers

Suggested answer could include the following:

1. What are the main issues raised and how are these impacting the community?

- There are noise complaints made against the local church on a Tuesday evening every week from 7pm to 10pm.
- This has caused one local resident to aggressively confront the church congregation during service, threatening arson.
- There are also complaints regarding rubbish littered across the road on Wednesday mornings from the night before.
- Vehicles of church attendees are causing parking issues for the local residents.
- One of the local residents of South Town, who is also a church goer, has been harassed by local teenagers.
- Overall, the current issues are causing rising tension between the church and the local residents and could easily escalate if action is not taken.

2. Provide your recommendations on how we can resolve these issues?

- There are a number of concerns here which need to be addressed. The noise issue, the parking, the littering, the harassment, and the aggression shown by the resident threatening to burn down the church.
- You could suggest that the church members are contacted, as they may not be aware of the noise coming from the church and the effect this is having on the surrounding residents. Once aware, they could take actions to prevent any further noise issues or reduce to an acceptable level.
- With regards to the parking, we should collaborate with the council to see if putting resident permit parking in the road will prevent further parking issues. However, this may have an impact on the churchgoers, so you could speak to them also to see if members of the church are able to car share/

walk to the church, to reduce the number of vehicles used by the congregation.

- The rubbish issue could be alleviated by the church if there are designated bins, this would prevent animals ripping open the rubbish bags. You could suggest to the reverend that he needs to put his rubbish in bins rather than leaving it outside in bin bags.
- The harassment needs to be dealt with and you should speak to the victim to offer support to see if they can identify the culprits so further action can be taken.
- Hold a meeting with the council, the church and the residents to discuss the issues amicably and present your resolutions. This will help ease tensions between the residents and the church. It is also important to tackle the harassment, threats and aggression. Make clear that any further occurrences will be dealt with according to the law.
- Set up a channel of communication within the community so Church-goers and residents can amicably discuss any future issues at the first instance.

3. How will these recommendations have a positive impact on the community?

- By showing impartiality and being aware of the issues faced by both the residents and the churchgoers, the resolutions will help to ensure both parties feel they have been heard and understood. This is imperative to ease tensions and provide a common ground for both the residents and the church.
- By hosting the meeting with the council, you are taking ownership of the issues. This allows a platform for all to share their concerns and provides the opportunity for the police and council to answer the points raised which should in turn ease tensions between the church and the local residents.
- It is important that diversity is encouraged within the community and noone is discriminated against. Relationships within the community will improve if everyone feels supported.

4. Are there any potential risks to the community?
   - The aggression and harassment shown to the church-goers could result in members of the church no longer taking part in the congregation, as they may no longer feel safe. Although this may suit the residents, as a police officer you must remain impartial and as the church congregation is part of the community, this would be a negative outcome to the issue.
   - If the council decided to make the area resident only parking this could cause the church congregation to park elsewhere and cause similar issues in neighbouring streets.

5. What can be done to provide reassurance for the community?
   - To monitor the situation to ensure all recommendations are implemented and working effectively, we should patrol the area on a Tuesday evening and follow up with residents and the church goers to ensure there are no further incidents or issues.
   - Hold a follow up meeting with the council, church and residents to ensure everybody is happy with the current implemented actions and give everyone the opportunity to offer their feedback.
   - Provide a dedicated phone line to contact police or council to report any further incidents or for advice.
   - As the churchgoers are members of the community, their needs must be met equally and you must ensure they are safe and treated without prejudice.

Written Exercise 6

To: PC Jones

From: Sergeant Smith

Subject: Speeding and reckless driving in Littleshire village

Date: 11.07.2020

Morning PC Jones,

We have been made aware of a potentially dangerous occurrence in the village of Littleshire. There seems to be an increased number of incidents of speeding and reckless driving along the narrow and winding roads of the village. The most recent almost resulted in a head-on collision between the speeding vehicle and oncoming vehicle heading in the opposite direction.

Along with the members of the local community, we are becoming increasingly concerned that this could result in further near misses or worse.

Littleshire, sits equally 1.5 miles between the main town of Ficshire and a further 1.5 miles to a newly built industrial estate on the outskirts of Lionhare. According to the local vicar in Littleshire, since the new industrial estate opened, the village has seen a large increase in vehicles using the roads to travel to the new industrial area.

I have attached a number of documents for your perusal and to assist you.

1. What are the main issues raised and how are these issues impacting the community?
2. Provide your recommendations on how we can resolve these issues?
3. How will these recommendations have a positive impact on the community?
4. Are there any potential risks to the community?
5. What can be done to provide reassurance for the community?

Attachment 1: Map of the local routes

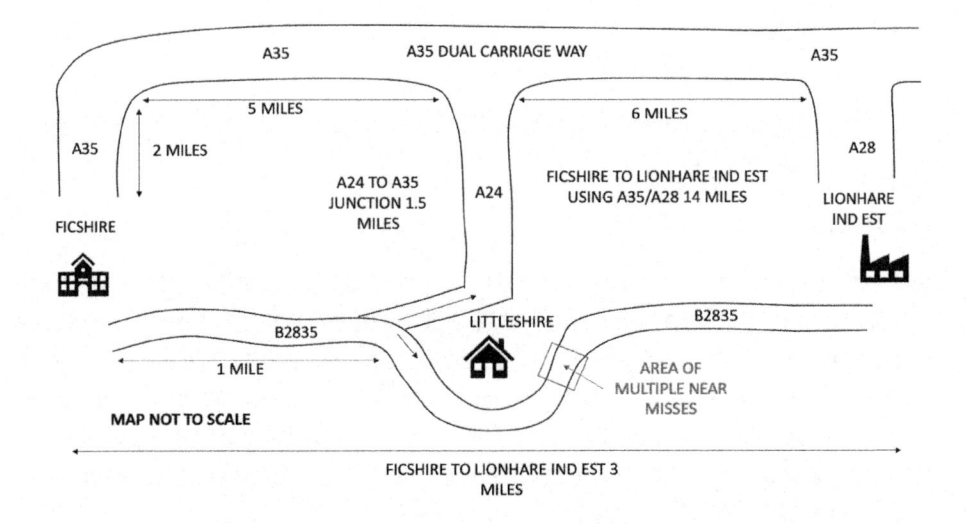

```
                        A35        A35 DUAL CARRIAGE WAY              A35
                    ←—— 5 MILES ——→        ←——— 6 MILES ———→
       A35                                                              A28
        ↑      2 MILES
        ↓              A24 TO A35          FICSHIRE TO LIONHARE IND EST
                       JUNCTION 1.5   A24  USING A35/A28 14 MILES       LIONHARE
    FICSHIRE           MILES                                            IND EST
       🏠                                                                🏭

                           B2835        LITTLESHIRE        B2835
                      ←—— 1 MILE ——→        🏠
                                                         AREA OF
            MAP NOT TO SCALE                          MULTIPLE NEAR
                                                         MISSES

                             FICSHIRE TO LIONHARE IND EST 3
                                         MILES
```

Attachment 2: Eyewitness statement regarding the near miss in Littleshire.

I was walking back home from the village shop at 15:41 on the 08.07.2020. As I was about to cross the road two cars, which seemed to be racing each other, sped past me. They must have been doing at least 70mph. I know this because we have the speed indicators which warn drivers of the speed they are doing. This is crazy, as the limit along the narrow roads is only 50mph, which is way too fast anyway in my opinion. It is a good job I had my wits about me as I could have quite easily been run over by these idiots!

Something needs to be done, before someone gets seriously hurt or worse. Since this industrial estate has opened this has been a common occurrence. These roads are not suitable for the amount of traffic.

Attachment 3: Report of reckless driving along the B2835.

"I was travelling home from work on Monday afternoon. I work in Ficshire, and live in Lionhare. I usually take the B2835, which goes through the picturesque village of Littleshire. I like taking this route as this is usually a nice quiet road and is much shorter than taking the A35 to Lionhare.

As I was driving around a sharp bend, just leaving Littleshire village, I was confronted by two vehicles which seemed to be racing each other. Seeing this, I had to take evasive action and mount the path to avoid the oncoming car in the wrong lane. Luckily, there was no one on the path otherwise this could have caused a nasty accident. I have noticed over the last few weeks since the new industrial estate has opened, that the B2835 has been a lot busier.

Attachment 4: Complaint to the Highways Agency regarding the A35 road condition.

To Whom It May Concern,

My name is Liam Harris, I live in Lionhare, and travel to work each day down the A35 to my place of work in Ficshire. The reason I am writing to you today is to complain regarding the state of the road surface, which is shockingly bad and although this has been the case for a while, not a lot seems to have been done.

The road has been in a state of disrepair for the last 3 months and it is becoming quite annoying with the number of potholes appearing in the road on both carriageways. This is also is having an excessive effect on the wear and tear of my vehicle, as I have already had to replace two tyres due to driving over these unavoidable potholes. I have recently also had my car's MOT done and the mechanic informed me that my shock absorbers will need to be replaced. When I asked him if the cause could be the A35's road condition, he stated; 'Stay well clear of the A35, that's what has caused the damage' and recommended I find an alternate route.

Can someone please advise if there are any plans to do anything about the state of the road. after all, we should be able travel to work without the risk of damaging our vehicles due to the state of the roads. Also, with regards to the damage to my car, I would like to claim compensation as the mechanic believes that the excessive wear to my vehicle is likely due to the condition of the A35.

I await your reply.

Mr L. Harris.

[Reply from Highways Agency Officer]

Dear Mr Harris,

Thank you for your email and bringing this matter to our attention.

We are very sorry to hear of the concerns you have highlighted regarding the state of the A35 road. We are aware of the issues you have raised and the route is due to be completely resurfaced in October (3 months from now). We are very sorry for the delay, however, our highways team are currently working to complete the nearby M9 motorway junction resurfacing which is currently due to finish in the last week of September.

Once this is complete, it is our intention to start work on the A35 repairs, unless we have other emergency repairs that need dealing with urgently, as this would take priority over the A35. The reason we class this road as a lower priority is because there are other suitable routes which connect the two towns such as the B2835 which passes through Littleshire. To save further wear to your vehicle in the interim, I would recommend the B2835 route.

With regards to the damage to your vehicle, you will need to contact the road compliance compensation team at the following email address claims@highways_Ficshire.gov.uk and they will send a form for you to complete.

I hope this helps,

Brian King

Highways customer care.

YOUR ANSWER / NOTES

Written Exercise 6 Answers

Suggested answer could include the following:

1. What are the main issues raised and how are these impacting the community?

- There are a number of issues; The most pressing is the dangerous driving which has a resulted in a number of near misses. The safety of the pedestrians and road users is paramount.
- The route is a narrow B road which seems unsuitable for large volumes of traffic, which has seen an increase since the new industrial estate was opened just outside Lionhare.
- An alternate longer route is available along the A35, but the road condition is poor.
- This is more than likely causing commuters to travel along the B2835 to avoid the A35.

2. Provide your recommendations on how we can resolve these issues?

- You should collaborate with the Highways Agency to add Speed calming components in the village to prevent road users speeding along the road. As a matter of urgency speed cameras, speed bumps and CCTV, should be installed.
- Add warning signs in the area of multiple incidents to warn drivers of the sharp bend.
- Add traffic lights to an area on a straight section of the road where it is safe for pedestrians to cross and road users have clear vision of the road.
- Patrol cars to be parked to observe and catch any drivers found to be speeding or driving recklessly and prosecuted as per current law.
- As a direct result of the issues, it is probable that many road users are using the B2835 to avoid the A35, due to the potential damage to their vehicles. Due to this you

should suggest to the Highways agency, that this needs to be scheduled immediately as an emergency because of the potential danger to residents and other road users in Littleshire.
- Suggest to the Highways agency that the speed limit needs lowering to help avoid any potential incidents/accidents.
- As stated in attachment 4 the Highways agency seem to be actively informing road users to take the B2835 as an alternate route. Take ownership and contact the highways agency to ask them to stop recommending the route due to the dangers caused by the increased traffic.
- You could suggest an alternate route, which eliminates part of the A35, but also diverts traffic away from Littleshire. B2835/A24/A35

3. How will these recommendations have a positive impact on the community?
- By taking these actions you are taking ownership to provide a safer environment for the residents and the road users.
- Adding the traffic calming elements, will have a direct impact by helping to prevent any further potential incidents.
- The patrol vehicles will help to catch and prosecute any dangerous speeding drivers.
- By collaborating with highways agency to bring forward the priority of the A35 repairs to be an emergency status, this will provide confidence that the repairs will be completed in a timely manner, which in turn will reduce the volume of traffic using the B2835.
- By informing the Highways agency to not recommend the B2835 as an alternate route you are helping to prevent further vehicles using the route.
- The alternate route, B2835/A24/A35 could help to minimise the impact of vehicles using the A35 as they would only be travelling on part of the road.

4. Are there any potential risks to the community?

- You could suggest that the traffic calming elements will not be welcome to all.
- The calming elements, could cause congestion for local road users.
- It is possible that some commuters will still use the B2835 as the travelling distance is greatly reduced as opposed to the A35 route, therefore some element of risk will remain.

5. What can be done to provide reassurance for the community?

- You could suggest holding a meeting the Highways agency and the Littleshire community, to communicate on the actions being taken by the Police and the highways agency to minimise the risk of incidents/accidents. Listen to any further concerns raised and act upon these.
- You also need to address the concerns of the commuters, regarding the A35 damages. Working together with the highways agency and advise of the impending repair work to be undertaken as an emergency and what measure will be undertaken to minimise the impact on commuters
- You should also communicate to the local residents that any speeding drivers caught will be prosecuted, but you are confident that the measures put in place will reduce any incidents greatly, but pedestrians should remain vigilant for any hazards.

Written Exercise 7

To: PC Jones

From: Sergeant Smith

Subject: Anti-Social Behaviour in the Town Centre

Date: 23.10.2020

Morning PC Jones,

As you are aware after this morning's briefing, there have been a number of issues recently in the town centre with regards to large groups of teenagers, riding around on skateboards. On a couple of occasions there have been accidents when the skateboarders have lost control and fallen into oncoming pedestrians. In one case, the collision resulted in a broken ankle to one of the pedestrians. After speaking to a number of shoppers and workers in the high street, it is clear that this issue has escalated over the last two weeks due to the closure of the Formation Skate Park for refurbishments. Formation Skate Park plans to reopen in January 2021.

Town centre users, shopkeepers, and passers-by are growing frustrated with these issues as they have not seen any response from the council. We have also received a complaint from a parent regarding aggressive behaviour which was directed towards his son.

Before this escalates further, we need to investigate and address the concerns of the community. I have attached a number of supporting documents, which will be of assistance. Can you please address the following concerns?

1. What are the main issues raised and how are these issues impacting the community?
2. Provide your recommendations on how we can resolve these issues?
3. How will these recommendations have a positive impact on the community?
4. Are there any potential risks to the community?
5. What can be done to provide reassurance for the community?

Attachment 1: Statement taken from a resident regarding skateboarders in town centre.

"I was doing my shopping in the town centre yesterday afternoon. I was walking past the clock tower when I was nearly decapitated by a lad on a skateboard, who was attempting to jump on his board from the top of the steps on the clock tower. I have noticed in the last couple of weeks an increase of kids on skateboards around the town centre, surely this isn't the right place for this activity!"

Attachment 2: Complaint from Mr Collings regarding aggressive behaviour towards his son.

I want to report some aggressive behaviour which was aimed at my son. He was walking through the town centre on Saturday with his mates – they head into town to grab food before going to hang out at Formation. He was approached and grabbed by a man who threatened to beat him up if he didn't get out of the town centre now. According to my son this was a fully-grown man. How brave he must be, picking on kids! If something is not done to stop this, I will be down there next Saturday and if I find him there will be trouble.

Attachment 3: Complaint from a shop keeper regarding teenagers congregating near her boutique.

Dear Sir/Madam,

I am writing to you today about the increased number of teenagers loitering in the town centre.

My name is Maria Pearson, and I am the owner of MP's Boutique which is based in the town centre, near the clock tower. Recently there has been an increased presence of youths hanging around outside my shop acting suspiciously. I must admit that I have not seen them do anything wrong but I do believe their presence is having a detrimental impact on customers visiting my store.

It's definitely impacting my sales, so can anything be done about this?

Many thanks, Maria.

Attachment 4: Community PCSO report on an incident in the town centre

Incident report: 2743, Date 21.10.2020, 13:23.

At approximately 12:45 I was patrolling the town centre, when I was approached by a gentleman who informed me that his wife had been knocked over by a young girl on a skateboard. When I arrived at the scene, I could see that the lady was conscious, but seemed to be in a fair amount of pain. I noticed that she had some minor cuts to her forehead so I called an ambulance right away.

The person on the skateboard had fled but left their skateboard at the scene. Once the paramedics arrived, they examined the lady and discovered there were no head injuries, but she had suffered a broken ankle from the fall. As a result, she was then taken to hospital in the ambulance for further treatment.

I took the details of the husband so I could contact him and his wife later regarding the incident, I then patrolled the immediate area to locate any witnesses. Although no one came forward who had witnessed the incident, I did hear from many people that there has been an increase in the number of teenagers using the area as a halfpipe. This seems to be a consequence of the local skate park being closed by the council whilst they undertake some urgent repairs.

YOUR ANSWER / NOTES

Written Exercise 7 Answers

Suggested answer could include the following:

1. What are the main issues raised and how are these impacting the community?

- It is understood that groups of teenagers are hanging around the town centre on skateboards. They are causing disruption to the nearby shops and town centre users and there have been accidents resulting in injuries.

- On one occasion a member of the public was injured when one of the skateboarders collided with them.

- Shopkeepers are concerned about the impact the teenagers hanging around the town centre is having on their sales and have reported less shoppers are using their stores and the town centre.

- A member of the public has possibly confronted a teenager in the town centre and threatened them. This has also prompted their parent to respond with threats to avenge the behaviour against his son.

- It could be suggested that the influx of skateboarders and youths hanging around the town centre, could be because of the closure of the skate park.

2. Provide your recommendations on how we can resolve these issues?

- As a police officer it is your duty to support the local communities. With this in mind it is vital that the safety of the local community is protected as much as possible. As reported, there have been a number of incidents, and one injury, this is a clear indication that using skateboards should not be permitted in the town centre, and this must be addressed.

- Collaborate with the local council to have signs erected stating that the use of skateboards is not to be permitted due to health and safety concerns.

- Increase patrols to ensure that the new rules are followed.
- Speak to the other shopkeepers to analyse if any of the other shops are experiencing issues which are impacting their business and sales.
- Collaborate with the council to determine a different location the skateboarders can use. The closed facility is not due to open until Jan 2021, which is several months away so a new location in the interim should alleviate the presence of skateboarders in the town centre. This will also show impartiality as you are actively trying to find a solution for all.
- You should offer support to the person injured and work with them to try to identify the person who pushed them over.
- Speak to the parent of the boy who was threatened, explain the issues which have been experienced in the town centre as he may not be aware. Show support, and state you will do everything necessary to find the person responsible. Seek to inspire by forewarning the father of the dangers of him taking the law into his own hands and the consequences which could result in any such action.

3. How will these recommendations have a positive impact on the community?
- By implementing the ban on using skateboards in the town, you are actively taking measures to increase the safety of the community so no further accidents will occur.
- The extra patrols will provide the community that the police are actively working to reduce the issues and support the community.
- By collaborating with the council to try to find an alternative location where people can use their skateboards you are addressing the needs of the skateboarders too.
- By speaking to the shopkeepers, you are also seeking to ascertain if there are any issues which are resulting by teenagers hanging around their shops.

4. Are there any potential risks to the community?

- With the possible deterrents, it is possible the skateboarders will move to another location causing issues for the wider community.
- The extra patrols in the town centre may not be welcome to all.
- Some town centre users may still be discouraged from visiting.

5. What can be done to provide reassurance for the community?

- The patrols need to provide support to all members of the community. Explain the actions that are being put in place to keep the town centre safe and provide an alternate location for the skateboard community.
- Host joint meetings with the council to offer support to the community, explain the actions being taken and answer any queries raised.
- Monitor the situation and implement any further actions required.

Briefing Exercise 1

We've received an urgent call from the Site Manager of the Ficshire Music Festival which is currently taking place this weekend. They are reporting that the headline artist "Big Mo" has had his prized harmonica go missing under suspicious circumstances, despite always keeping it on his person. Earlier today Big Mo took part in a "meet and greet" session, and specifically requested no physical contact with fans, however numerous groups completely ignored this request and some even had the audacity to hug the star. The Site Manager is looking for swift action as Big Mo is now refusing to take to the stage until it is found. The news is filtering its way through to the crowds which are understandably growing frustrated, with some resorting to wildly throwing projectiles at the stage.

1. Highlight the issues that need addressing.
2. What are the consequences if the show doesn't go ahead?
3. What measures can be taken to reduce such incidents from occurring?
4. How do you address the no-contact request being breached?
5. What are your recommendations for addressing these issues?

NOTES

The Site Manager has called in again and is starting to take matters into his own hands. He is very angry and is threatening to stop all people from entering or leaving the festival site, until the missing harmonica is found. He shouted down the phone "if you don't find this stupid piece of metal I'll be ruined, and everyone will remember me as a failure, and it'll be all your fault!" We've also been informed by a reliable source that Big Mo clearly has no intentions of performing, as he has started watching a 6-hour film on his tour bus, which is displaying a "do not disturb" sign.

6. Does this new information change your initial thoughts and recommendations?
7. What's your next step in light of this new information?
8. How do you approach the Site Manager's behaviour?
9. How can you reassure the community?
10. What are the possible consequences of your proposed actions?

NOTES

We are receiving numerous reports that members of the general public have become injured by objects being hurled towards the stage in protest of Big Mo failing to perform. Some of the injuries are considered to be of a serious nature. The artist has since posted on social media "No harmonica. No show. My fee still gets paid." Officers at the scene have also reported that guests are now attempting to climb up the infrastructure of the site, and others are trying jump over walls to leave the hostile atmosphere. The Site Manager is nowhere to be seen.

11. Highlight the main issues that arise from this new information.
12. Does this information change your previous plan?
13. What is your next step in relation to contacting the Site Manager?
14. What concerns will this raise within the community?
15. Given how the events have unfolded, how would you change your initial approach to prevent this issue from escalating?

NOTES

YOUR ANSWER

Briefing Exercise 1 Answers

In your responses for questions 1-5 points you could have covered:

- Some of Big Mo's personal property has gone missing.
- Attendees of the festival are acting in dangerous manner in response to the news.
- The no-contact request made by the artist was ignored by the general public.
- If the event does not go ahead the behaviour of the crowd could escalate into a riot/protest.
- Apologise to Big Mo that his no contact request was ignored, being emotionally aware to why his motives for not performing.
- Reassure the attendees of the festival that this matter is being investigated thoroughly to ensure that Big Mo can perform as scheduled.
- Consider telling the Site Manager to position additional security/stewards nearby where projectiles are being thrown to deter this from happening.
- Consider discussing with Big Mo if he is still able to perform at the event without the harmonica to put a stop to the dangerous behaviour. Reassuring him that it is being looked into.
- Consider implementing a search protocol on entry and exit to the site.
- Consider conducting a search of the areas that Big Mo has been in since arriving at the site.

In your responses for questions 6-10 points you could have covered:

- The Site Manager is losing control of the situation and beginning to act off his own accord.
- How you will address the Site Manager's rude behaviour whilst being emotionally aware of the circumstances.
- Speak to the Site Manager calmly and effectively communicate that although you understand the gravity of the situation that he cannot stop attendees from leaving the site. But re-iterate that you will be conducting a search of all attendees before leaving.
- Big Mo is clearly not co-operating with this investigation. Consider obtaining a statement or further guidance from him.
- Consider an alternative act to perform in place of Big Mo in hope to control the crowd.
- The attendees may demand a refund if they don't get to see the artist they paid to see.
- Conducting searches may create a bottle-neck effective on entry/exit.
- Big Mo may become disgruntled by being replaced by an alternative act.

In your responses for questions 11-15 points you could have covered:

- Some attendees have been seriously injured by projectiles.
- The atmosphere has become hostile and is festering and creating further Health & Safety risks.
- Contact the Site Manager or a member of Big Mo's crew in aim to resolve the escalating situation.
- The event will receive a bad reputation for the events that have unfolded.
- The venue may decide not to hold such events of this nature in future out of concerns for the public both inside and outside of the site.
- Take ownership of the situation and consider shutting down the event to prevent further injuries regardless of the Site Manager's wishes.

Briefing Exercise 2

Yesterday we received a complaint from a local business owner residing in the Ficville Enterprise Park. Emma Pockets was concerned that an anti-feminist protest is taking place outside her business, and feels that the group have purposefully targeted her premises in the hope of triggering a reaction from the staff. Ms Pockets is opposed to the protest taking place as it strongly contradicts the company's values and beliefs, and her staff are looking to her to take action. One of her staff members has even threatened to take matters into their own hands by "showing them what a woman can really do". Other neighbouring businesses are also becoming concerned about the animosity of the protest and the negative impact it could have on footfall.

1. Highlight the issues that need addressing.
2. How do you respond to the protestors behaviour?
3. What can be done to reassure the businesses in the area?
4. How do you respond to the member of staff threatening to take action into their own hands?
5. What are your recommendations for addressing these issues?

NOTES

Unfortunately, as predicted, the protest has turned sour. As one member of staff arrived at the Ficville Enterprise Park this morning, the protestors were camped outside the entrance to "Big Cheesy Grins". The member of staff challenged the protestors in a rather abrupt manner and was subsequently met with a swarm of verbal abuse. The employee was enraged by this behaviour and snatched one of the signs made by the protestors, snapped it in half, and threw it to the ground in anger. In retaliation, one of the protestors pushed the employee to the floor, causing minor injuries. Shortly after this, an off-duty police officer waded in to calm the dispute. "Big Cheesy Grins" did not open for business due to this incident.

6. Does this new information change your initial thoughts and recommendations?
7. What's your next step in light of this new information?
8. How do you approach the employees behaviour?
9. How should you address the protestors blocking the entrance to "Big Cheesy Grins"?
10. What are the possible consequences of your proposed actions?

NOTES

We've received an anonymous tip that one of the protestors is the ex-husband of Emma Pockets. Sadly, the pair split last year due to Bryan's claims that Ms Pockets siphoned money from his personal and business accounts, to fund her own shop in Ficville Enterprise Park. Since their divorce Bryan has made it his sole purpose in life to seek revenge and has recruited all of the protestors under the illusion that it is an anti-feminist movement.

11. Highlight the main issues that arise from this new information.
12. Does this information change your previous plan?
13. What can be done to reassure the local businesses?
14. How do you approach informing the ex-wife of this information?
15. How do you think this will affect the wider community?

NOTES

YOUR ANSWER

Briefing Exercise 2 Answers

In your responses for questions 1-5 points you could have covered:

- The nature of the protest is considered discriminatory and should be disbanded.
- The staff members are looking for Ms Pockets to react to the situation, possibly in an aggressive or violent manner.
- The surrounding businesses are becoming agitated by the protest and may be drawn in to any disagreement, creating a more hostile environment.
- Take ownership of the situation and remove the anti-feminist protestors and assure them that you will deal with any concerns they may have about external behaviours impacting their shops.
- Advise Ms Pockets not to engage with the protestors and that by antagonising the protestors she will be escalating the issue not only for her business but the surrounding businesses too.
- Consider moving on the protest to an alternative location.
- Consider patrolling the area to ensure the protest is taking place in a peaceful manner.

In your responses for questions 6-10 points you could have covered:

- Considering the situation has escalated and your previous actions haven't deterred the protestors.

- Take ownership of the situation, challenge their behaviour and instruct them to disperse.

- Take a statement from the member of staff that was injured being emotionally aware of their injuries.

- Get in touch with the store managers in the area and collaborate with them to ensure this matter isn't escalated further and that staff members don't interact with the protestors.

- The protestors could move to another location and they could also become aggressive which is likely due to above escalation.

In your responses for questions 11-15 points you could have covered:

- The ex-husband has been potentially been a victim of theft. You should offer him guidance on how to pursue this matter legally and that the action of starting a protest is not the appropriate channel.
- Although there is now a clear motive for the protest being located at the Ficville Enterprise Park it still needs to be dealt with in the same manner.
- Deliver reports to the surrounding businesses on the incident that took place, what was actioned and how you will prevent any further recurrences.
- Do not approach Ms. Pockets about this new information. Only address her regarding the protest and advise her that it has been dealt with.
- This will discourage from the local community from shopping in this area, as they may be met with a confrontational atmosphere.
- This will also a negative impact on the businesses in the area if they were to see a reduction in footfall.
- Consider reaching out to the stores in the area and informing them that you are their to support with any matters of this kind and if they have any concerns to contact the police first.

Briefing Exercise 3

This afternoon we were contacted by a distressed pensioner to inform us that a large group of teenagers were congregating outside of his property playing football. He claimed that "the youths" in question were not only being very loud, but were also using very offensive language. Mr. Lewin stated that the ball had hit his kitchen window numerous times, and feared that it was only a matter of time before these "lay-abouts smash every window in the vicinity". The gentleman was clearly upset and was not only scared to challenge the group, but also afraid to leave his property.

1. Highlight the issues that need addressing.
2. What action do you take regarding the group of teenagers playing football?
3. What can be done to reassure Mr Lewin and the surrounding community?
4. What are the risks to yourself policing this incident?
5. What are your recommendations for addressing these issues?

NOTES

We have now received a fresh complaint from the groundskeeper that looks after the communal gardens that are outside Mr Lewin's property. He claims that the grass has been ripped to shreds, and two massive diverts have been made in the lawn. The groundskeeper also claims that he has been in contact with Mr Lewin, confirming that the group of teenagers were playing football, and completely ignored the "no ball games" sign, so Mr Lewin decided to challenge them. Mr Lewin has encouraged the groundskeeper to keep watch in case they return, and not to be afraid to use brute force to get the job done.

6. Does this new information change your initial thoughts and recommendations?

7. What's your next step in light of this new information?

8. How do you approach Mr Lewin over his comments about resolving the situation?

9. How should you address the "no ball games" sign being clearly ignored?

10. What issues are raised by Mr Lewin challenging the group, after initially being too scared to leave his home?

NOTES

This afternoon we have received a call from an angry parent claiming to be the mother of one of the children playing football. She claims her son was "brutally attacked" in an unprovoked manner by a grounds maintenance man. The son is covered in bruises on his legs and shins, plus he has a black eye. Mr Lewin claims to know nothing about an assault of any kind, but confirmed the teenagers were playing football again outside his property. The groundskeeper was off-duty at the time, he was on his lunch break and has denied all allegations.

11. Highlight the main issues that arise from this new information.

12. Does this information change your previous plan?

13. How do you address the son's injuries?

14. How can you reassure the mother that this matter will be resolved?

15. How does this incident change your approach to dealing with Mr Lewin and the groundskeeper?

NOTES

YOUR ANSWER

Briefing Exercise 3 Answers

In your responses for questions 1-5 points you could have covered:

- Mr Lewin is fearful that his property may be damaged. As a police officer you have a duty to serve the public, so this needs to be addressed.

- Mr Lewin is afraid to leave his property. You must take ownership of this situation by reassuring him that you will take the appropriate action to ensure he feels safe to leave his property.

- Mr Lewin has claimed that the group are acting in an anti-social manner which needs to be investigated further. It is imperative that you speak to the teenagers in question so that you have an accurate and impartial account of events.

- Ascertain whether or not the teenagers are permitted to be playing on the grounds. As a police officer you need to provide a solution for all parties involved.

- If ball games are permitted on the grounds, consider introducing a curfew, or only allocating a specific space to protect the nearby properties.

- If ball games are not permitted you will need to consider the visibility of signage and direct the public to alternative sites.

- Take ownership of the situation and work with the teenagers to provide an alternative location for them to play football.

- When approaching the group you and your colleague should stay together to ensure your collective safety.

- When conversing with the group it is important to adapt your communication accordingly to achieve a resolution.

- Reach out to other nearby residents and determine their views on the incident and if they have been impacted also.

In your responses for questions 6-10 points you could have covered:

- The communal gardens have been damaged and therefore immediate action needs to be taken to avoid further issues.
- The "no ball games" sign was ignored by the teenagers. As we have now established that ball games are prohibited, action needs to be taken to relocate the teenagers elsewhere, so that they aren't disturbing other members of the community.
- Consider introducing a penalty or fine if the "no ball games" is breached. Introduce extra signage to make this clear to the general public and also offer a telephone service to report such offences.
- Mr Lewin is encouraging the groundskeeper to take a potentially violent approach to dealing with the situation which must be discouraged. Warn him of the consequences of any such actions.
- Warn the teenagers of the consequences should they return to play ball games. Remember to adapt your approach demonstrating emotional awareness.
- Consider what actions need to be taken to rectify the damage to the gardens.
- Consider the potential consequences of the groundskeeper employing a physical approach. Advise the groundskeeper that any such actions are totally unacceptable.
- Mr Lewin feels that issue has not been resolved and although he was scared, he has felt the need to intervene himself, potentially putting himself at risk.
- The teenagers may react to Mr Lewin in a confrontational manner and aggravate the issue further.

In your responses for questions 11-15 points you could have covered:

- One of the youths has allegedly been attacked, which is likely to be in direct retaliation of the teenagers playing football in the communal gardens.

- The teenagers returned to the private gardens and once again ignored the "no ball games" sign. Consider their motive for returning to this site. As the signs have been ignored on multiple occasions, it would be appropriate to issue a penalty, and or fine to anyone found breaching these rules.

- The allegation of the assault needs to be investigated in accordance with the law.

- Consider the nature of the injuries sustained by the son. Is it plausible that the injuries sustained occurred from playing football?

- Consider what measures could be put in place to deter the youths from returning.

- You must be emotionally aware of the mothers concerns, but clearly state to her that her son was infringing upon the "no ball games"policy, and that the group had previously been warned not to play football at this location.

- Consider the likelihood that either Mr Lewin or the groundskeeper inflicted these injuries. You must speak to both parties to obtain an official statement regarding the alleged assault. You must consider the previous comments and behaviour of both parties also.

Briefing Exercise 4

We've received an angry email this morning from a shop owner, located in the centre of Ficshire High Street, stating that a member of the public is repeatedly performing obscenely loud music during peak shopping times. They've claimed to have challenged the musician on numerous occasions now, asking them to turn the volume down or to simply move on. Each time those requests have been met, however they simply turn up the next day with the same result. The shop owner stated, "I'm all for live music and enjoy buskers – it adds to the vibe. But surely they have to appreciate we have a business to run and that they could be potentially scaring away our paying customers!"

1. Highlight the issues that need addressing.
2. How do you respond to the busker's behaviour?
3. What measures can be taken to reduce such incidents from occurring?
4. What are the risks to yourself policing this incident?
5. What are your recommendations for addressing these issues?

NOTES

The busker has contacted us today to inform us that a member of the general public has damaged his portable speaker. He claims that he was counting his earnings for the day when all of a sudden a crazed female, approximately in her mid-30s, ran at full tilt down the high street and tripped over the speaker. The speaker went flying, and on impact with the ground it instantly smashed into hundreds of pieces. The female has injured her ankle and is very upset with the busker for placing such a cumbersome object in the street. She believes that the whole incident could've been avoided and there is no way she will pay to replace the smashed speaker. This created a massive scene outside the shop fronts, which definitely deterred some customers from shopping at the time.

6. Does this new information change your initial thoughts and recommendations?
7. What's your next step in light of this new information?
8. How do you deal with the female that has been injured?
9. Should the busker be allowed to perform during business hours in the high street?
10. How can you reassure the local businesses that this incident won't be repeated?

NOTES

After the scene was cleared the busker was speaking to one of the shop owners, apologising profusely for the disruption caused. He informed them that he recently lost his job and that if he can't scrape together £800 by the end of the month he'll be evicted from his rented accommodation. The musician had only recently secured a busking license and is now fully reliant on the earnings to make a living. The female that was injured in the incident is now considering taking legal action against the busker.

11. Highlight the main issues that arise from this new information.
12. Does this information change your previous plan?
13. What concerns might the local businesses have in light of this new information?
14. How do you approach the female that has been injured now that she is considering taking legal action?
15. How does the busker's financial predicament change your approach to dealing with this situation?

NOTES

YOUR ANSWER

Briefing Exercise 4 Answers

In your responses for questions 1-5 points you could have covered:

- A busker is performing in Ficshire High Street at an inconsiderate volume, and continues to repeat this behaviour.
- The shop owner is concerned that the busker is deterring potential customers from visiting their establishment.
- Check the musician has got a valid permit/license to perform in the area.
- Consider taking an open-minded approach when observing the busker and obtain a recording of the volume to check if it exceeds the legal standard.
- Reach out to other nearby business owners to see if they are also concerned by this matter.
- Respond to the complaint email, reassure the business owner by outlining the actions you plan to take to address the issue.
- Approach the busker and gain an understanding of why they continue to increase the volume of their performances. Inform them that a complaint has been raised and that if this continues the council may intervene.
- Is there a more appropriate place for the busker to move onto? Advise them that there are music venues in the area which may be more appropriate for live performances.
- There appears to be little to no risk to policing this incident as both parties have been relatively compliant and understanding of each others needs.

In your responses for questions 6-10 points you could have covered:

- An alternative location needs to be found for the busker to perform.
- The busker may be unable to perform without the portable speaker which may impede his ability to perform in such a setting.
- Obtain statements from the busker and the female who was injured to gain an understanding of the incident from both view points
- Obtain statements any witnesses of this incident. Ascertain whether the speaker was in a dangerous place, and was the female cautious when navigating the high street?
- Work collaboratively with the council, the local business owners and the busker to determine a resolution that all parties are happy with.
- Local businesses lost custom due to this incident occurring and may consider taking further actions against the musician.
- Consider allocating specific areas where such performances are permitted where there is appropriate space.
- You have to be impartial and open-minded when dealing with the busker and the injured female.

In your responses for questions 11-15 points you could have covered:

- Be emotionally aware that the busker is now unable to perform and needs to seek an alternative method of financial security.
- The busker is aware of the impact this incident has had on local businesses and has apologised.
- The busker may have no option but to continue to perform in the area, which may not be problematic if it is not at such a loud volume. This may be of some concern to local businesses in case similar incidents may occur.
- You must be emotionally aware of the busker's financial position, but it's important not to treat him more or less favourably due to this new information.
- Respond to the incident as normal, collecting any statements from witnesses. This may be required should the female pursue legal action.

Briefing Exercise 5

Early this morning we received a hand-written message from an anonymous local resident of Ficshire who has reported an influx of graffiti on residents properties and external walls. They've also included photographs of the offences, which all seem to include the tag "Fruit Bat". The graffiti is rather tasteful, but nevertheless this issue needs to be dealt with. After a quick glance over the images, it is clear that these offences are concentrated in the South West Ficshire area, which is known to be rife with gangs that are always tussling for territory.

1. Highlight the issues that need addressing.
2. What concerns will the above raise within the community?
3. What measures can be taken to reduce such incidents from occurring?
4. What can be done to reassure the community?
5. What are your recommendations for addressing these issues?

NOTES

There has now been a surge of these tags appearing all over Ficshire which has triggered a series of local schools to launch a fundraising event to help pay for the removal of the graffiti. However, some residents are upset by this proposal as they think the tags are actually rather tasteful and add to the character of the town. Some have even claimed that since having their property tagged that it has increased their house price. As of yet there has been no evidence or suggestion as to the identity of "Fruit Bat", nor has the tag been confirmed to be linked to any local gang or gang related activity.

6. Does this new information change your initial thoughts and recommendations?
7. What's your next step in light of this new information?
8. How do you deal with the residents that are opposing this fundraising event?
9. How do you approach the schools to inform them of those opposing the fundraiser?
10. How can you reassure the residents of Ficshire and the surrounding communities that this won't spread further?

NOTES

The fundraiser arranged by local schools was cancelled due to an outcry of public support for the street art, however in just a few days we have seen an unprecedented spike in the level of graffiti all over Ficshire. Many other "artists" are now getting involved and the whole town is starting to look like one giant sketchbook. Unfortunately, it's not all tasteful either, as some of the tags are becoming deeply offensive, using coarse or even racist language. We've also received reports of empty spray paint cans being hurled at passing traffic, with one incident injuring a cyclist.

11. Highlight the main issues that arise from this new information.
12. Does this information change your previous plan?
13. How might local creatives feel about the removal of the street art?
14. How can you revive interest in the fundraiser proposed by local schools?
15. What are the potential consequences of removing only some of the tags, as opposed to all of the graffiti?

NOTES

YOUR ANSWER

Briefing Exercise 5 Answers

In your responses for questions 1-5 points you could have covered:

- There has been an influx of graffiti appearing on private property around Ficshire which needs to be removed.
- If the matter isn't dealt with swiftly it could encourage further damages.
- The community may become concerned that the graffiti is encouraging/promoting gang culture.
- There might be concerns about the lack of respect being shown towards their properties.
- Consider deploying additional patrols in the South West region of Ficshire.
- Introduce anti-vandalism deterrents such as CCTV or extra street lights.
- Distribute flyers to residents informing them of the offences and reminding them to be vigilant of any similar acts taking place.
- Consider implementing a collaborative campaign with a neighbourhood watch or similar society.

In your responses for questions 6-10 points you could have covered:

- Due to the lack of evidence to suggest that the graffiti is associated with any form of gang culture, your approach to this issue may change.
- As some residents have come out in support of the graffiti and want to keep it, you will need to remind the residents of Ficshire that it is in fact a criminal offence, regardless of the motive. However, in the event a resident wishes to keep any graffiti on their private property, they are able to do so, but it cannot damage anyone else's property, nor can it be deemed offensive/discriminatory to any community.
- You must remain impartial to any for/against campaigns for keeping the street art.
- Consider collaborating with the school fundraising event and offer workshops on the value of keeping where you live clean and tidy.
- You must notify the schools that not all residents are in full support of their fundraising campaign. Work with them to offer incentives for taking part in the event and explain alternative motives/view-points for wanting to remove the graffiti, or simply allocate a new location for such art.
- You must inform all residents of Ficshire that you are investigating this spike in graffiti and are taking additional measures to help prevent further incidents from occurring. This can be the introduction of more patrols and CCTV in the local and surrounding communities, plus detailing any plans to get the graffiti removed. By doing so, the offenders will also be made aware that they are more likely to get caught if they continue to repeat this act.

In your responses for questions 11-15 points you could have covered:

- Consider the impact of the public support for wanting to keep the graffiti. Could it have encouraged further offences to be committed?
- Due to the fundraiser being cancelled the impetus to clean up Fichsire has been delayed significantly.
- The litter and injured cyclist needs to be addressed. Obtain a statement from the cyclist to try and gain an insight as to who the possible offender is.
- The school and the local residents may feel conflicted due to the recent events. Consider measures to boost local morale and improve relationships, stressing the importance of collaboration to achieve collective goals.
- Local artists may feel unfairly treated if some of their street art is removed, but others are left. Therefore, a more universal approach must be applied by removing all graffiti unless consent is denied.
- Explain to local artists that there are alternative methods of displaying such pieces of work, without damaging private property. Create a space in the town specifically for artists to display their work.
- As the rate of graffiti is escalating patrols must be increased and anyone caught committing the act should be issued with a penalty/fine.
- The content of graffiti is also becoming more outspoken and more divisive. Therefore, such pieces should be removed as a priority to avoid damaging or upsetting any members of the community.
- You may also want to put up signs in highly affected areas stating that anyone caught damaging private property will be penalised.

Briefing Exercise 6

We received a call this evening from Mrs Rupinder who wanted to voice her concerns about a dispute currently underway in Jasper's Drive between two neighbours. She claims that the two neighbours are having heated arguments at all hours of the day over the ownership of a small plot of land that runs across the back of their rear gardens. The land is becoming increasingly overgrown and both parties are accusing the other of neglecting it. It's really damaging the community spirit and some people living nearby are starting to take sides which is making matters worse.

1. Highlight the issues that need addressing.
2. What concerns will the above raise within the community?
3. What impact could leaving the land unmaintained have on the community?
4. What involvement should Mrs Rupinder have in the resolution?
5. What are your recommendations for addressing these issues?

NOTES

We have been informed that one of the neighbours caught up in this dispute is the son of the homeowner, Harvey Jakobson. His mother, Emilia Jakobson, is gravely ill resulting her being unable to leave the property. Mr Jakobson is under an immense amount of pressure and is struggling to cope with the additional stress caused by this ongoing dispute over the unkept land. Their neighbours, the Lookmans' are threatening to take legal action if this matter isn't resolved urgently. The Lookmans' have made it clear that they have little to no concern for the consequences of their actions.

6. Does this new information change your initial thoughts and recommendations?
7. What's your next step in light of this new information?
8. How do you deal with the neighbours that are not being emotionally aware of the situation?
9. How do you approach Mr Jakobson?
10. What alternative measures could you suggest to resolve this matter?

NOTES

The land has been identified as being the property of Emilia Jakobsons. She has written to the Lookmans' stating that she doesn't have the ability, time or resources to tend to the plot. Upon receiving this news the Lookmans' have decided to claim the plot for themselves, moving their boundary fence to incorporate the plot, and have listed their property for sale with the additional plot included as part of their garden

11. Highlight the main issues that arise from this new information.
12. How does this new information change your previous plan?
13. What action should be taken considering the Lookmans' behaviour to claim the land as their own?
14. How might this series of events impact the neighbours who were also getting brought into this dispute?
15. What motivations might the Jakobsons' have had for writing the note to the Lookmans'?

NOTES

YOUR ANSWER

Briefing Exercise 6 Answers

In your responses for questions 1-5 points you could have covered:

- Two neighbours are having a dispute over the ownership and upkeep of a plot of land.

- The commotion is impacting other nearby residents and the matter is escalating.

- Consider the implications of the plot of land falling into further disrepair, making it an eye saw and increasingly more dangerous.

- Mrs Rupinder does not need any further involvement in this matter, you should inform her that you are working with the neighbours to achieve a resolution and provide contact information which she, or any other neighbour, can use in the event the situation escalates.

- Advise both parties that they must seek out contractually who has ownership of the land. It is crucial that you remain impartial when trying to diffuse tensions.

- If the land is left to fall into further disrepair this dispute could escalate and more drastic measures may be required to relieve tensions. This could also have a negative impact on house prices in the immediate vicinity as the land may become dangerous or an environmental issue.

- Collaborate with the local council and the neighbours to arrange for a third party to come in and maintain the land as a one-off service. Once that has been acted upon, advise the neighbours that they must seek who has ownership of the land.

In your responses for questions 6-10 points you could have covered:

- The ownership of the land still needs to be determined, this should not change your recommendation that both neighbours should seek confirmation of who owns the land.
- You must be emotionally aware of the situation and the additional stress when approaching Mr Jakobson. Offer assistance and solutions to resolve the dispute such as where to find local garden maintenance services.
- You must approach the Lookmans' and advise them that this dispute is causing Mr Jakobson distress and that he is also looking to resolve the matter. Recommend that they explore alternative methods to resolve the issue. Find out what their motive is for such drastic actions.
- Suggest a third party to come in and maintain the land, with the two neighbours splitting the costs.
- Suggest that both parties contact their local authority and determine who has ownership of the land. Once concluded do they want the land? Would they consider selling the land?

Police Officer Online Assessment Tests

In your responses for questions 11-15 points you could have covered

- The Jakobsons' have ownership of the land but do not have the time/resources to maintain it.
- The Lookmans' claimed the land, even though it is not lawfully theirs.
- The Lookmans' are falsely advertising their property to include this land.
- The surrounding neighbours may also decide to intervene considering the actions of the Lookmans'. This could escalate matters from a verbal to a physical altercation if not handled carefully.
- You must instruct the Lookmans' to re-instate the boundary to it's previous location. You may suggest to them if they do wish to claim ownership of the land that they enquire with the Jakobsons' to see if they would be open to selling the plot.
- Provide support and advice to the Jakobsons' so they can maintain the land which is part of their property. Suggest that if it is too much of a workload to take on that they could sell the land.
- The Jakobsons' are looking to solve the dispute amicably, by explaining why they have been unable to maintain the land. They have also indicated that this situation is unlikely to change and therefore have decided to reach out to the Lookmans'. However, they have not explicitly offered the land to the Lookmans' and therefore this matter needs to be addressed.

Briefing Exercise 7

We've received numerous reports from Ficville council that the amount of wheelie bins going missing has sky-rocketed in the past month. In the previous six months, on average two wheelie bins would go missing each month. However, this month they've processed 34 missing bin replacement requests. There has been some unrest in the community at the escalating price of replacing these bins, but such demand like this is totally unprecedented. One claimant declared that they thought they saw someone run off with it in the early hours of the morning and load it into a van, but were unable to take note of the vehicle registration. Understandably, the victims are extremely unhappy with having to deal with this unexpected expense and the council are growing concerned that something nefarious is occurring.

1. Highlight the issues that need addressing.
2. What concerns will the above raise within the community?
3. What measures can be taken to reduce such incidents from occurring?
4. What can be done to reassure the community?
5. What are your recommendations for addressing these issues?

NOTES

We've received confirmation that a large quantity of wheelie bins have been found on a nearby building site, with some in a very poor condition, but the majority are pristine. The unit is owned by Fergus McConnolly, founder of "Ficville's Helping Hand". We have temporarily seized the bins as evidence, until we receive further instruction. At the time of the discovery nobody was present at premises, but a large stack of flyers from the company advertising "man with a van services" were visible. The flyers offer numerous odd jobs and services at a reasonable price, but most notably include being able to provide and collect wheelie bins on behalf of the council.

6. Does this new information change your initial thoughts and recommendations?
7. What's your next step in light of this new information?
8. How can you verify that this is a legitimate service being offered?
9. How might this discovery impact the communities trust in Mr McConnolly's business and the local council?
10. What impact will this have on "Ficville's Helping Hand"?

NOTES

Mr McConnolly has been in contact and is irate that the wheelie bins from his premises have been seized. He explained that he received permission from the council to provide this service and without it his business will fall into serious financial difficulties. He begged us to release the bins, sobbing throughout his statement. However, after contacting the council they stated that they gave explicit permission for "Ficville's Helping Hand" to carry out repairs on the bins but no other services were authorised.

11. Highlight the main issues that arise from this new information.
12. How does this new information change your previous plan?
13. What must you consider when dealing with Mr McConnolly's request?
14. How could this situation have been handled better?
15. What fallout will there be for the wider community if this matter is unresolved?

NOTES

Briefing Exercise 7 Answers

In your responses for questions 1-5 points you could have covered:

- Residents of Ficville have had their wheelie bins stolen or go missing. Thus resulting them in having to pay for replacements.
- The community are growing unsettled by the rising prices of the bins.
- The Ficville council may be struggling to keep up with such unforeseen demand, thus resulting in uncollected waste.
- Consider sending out flyers to the public, notifying them of such incidents. Ask them to remain vigilant and inform them of anything suspicious.
- Invite collaboration with any local businesses/residents to submit CCTV footage in hope to resolve the matter.
- Recommend bin locks and/or number stickers so that residents can identify their bins.
- Ask the council to collate a report of all the residents that are requesting replacement bins. Establish if there is a pattern to the events.

In your responses for questions 6-10 points you could have covered:

- This new information will not change your approach to the investigation. However, you may consider contacting those that have had bins go missing and inform them that progress is being made on the case. Ask the victims if their bins had any identifiable qualities so that you can return any that match the description.

- Contact the council to verify if such services were approved by them.

- Obtain a statement from Fergus McConnolly, clarifying his services and if he has obtained official approval to do so.

- Consider the likelihood of Ficville's Helping Hand operating in a fraudulent manner.

- You must be transparent with Mr McConnolly when informing him why the bins were seized.

- You must be impartial and consider all circumstantial evidence before taking any further action.

- This discovery may have detrimental impact on relations between the community and the council. They may perceive this incident to be caused by the council handing out contracts to businesses which aren't trustworthy, or fit for delivering the service. Review with the council what measures are in place when qualifying outsourcing such work.

- Ficville's Helping Hand will be unable to trade until this matter is fully investigated. They will also be unable to resume any repairs on the bins which they already have. This mas result in residents missing waste collection days, potentially leading to a rise in animals opening rubbish sacks and litter being spread.

In your responses for questions 11-15 points you could have covered:

- Mr McConolly did not have permission to be removing any resident's bins, with or without their consent.
- The survival of Mr McConolly's business is dependent on the return of the wheelie bins.
- You must be emotionally aware of Mr McConnolly's financial situation, but not treat him differently due to this discovery.
- You must inform Mr McConnolly that you have contacted the council and they have not given his business permission to provide/collect wheelie bins on behalf of the council, only to restore damaged ones.
- Consider requesting the customer information of the wheelie bins which are held. Can Mr McConnolly produce this information? If not, how did he source them?
- With the matter unresolved, the community may still be missing their wheelie bins, causing issues for waste collection and potential environmental hazards.
- There has been some miscommunication between the Mr McConnolly and the council as to the agreement they made. Could measures have put in place to ensure that the services agreed were made more clear?
- Consider a possible motive for Mr McConnolly acquiring and selling these goods without permission.

You have now reached the end of the testing guide and no doubt you will be ready to take the online assessment tests. The majority of candidates who pass the police officer selection process have a number of common attributes. These are as follows:

1. They believe in themselves.

The first factor is self-belief. Regardless of what anyone tells you, you can become a police officer. Just like any job of this nature, you have to be prepared to work hard in order to be successful. Make sure you have the self-belief to pass the selection process and fill your mind with positive thoughts.

2. They prepare fully.

The second factor is preparation. Those people who achieve in life prepare fully for every eventuality and that is what you must do when you apply to become a police officer. Work very hard and especially concentrate on your weak areas.

3. They persevere.

Perseverance is a fantastic word. Everybody comes across obstacles or setbacks in their life, but it is what you do about those setbacks that is important. If you fail at something, then ask yourself 'why' you have failed. This will allow you to improve for next time and if you keep improving and trying, success will eventually follow. Apply this same method of thinking when you apply to become a police officer.

4. They are self-motivated.

How much do you want this job? Do you want it, or do you really want it? When you apply to join the police you should want it more than anything in the world. You levels of self-motivation will shine through on your application and during your interview. For the weeks and months leading up to the police officer selection process, be motivated as best you can and always keep your fitness levels up as this will serve to increase your levels of motivation.

Work hard, stay focused, and secure your dream career!

The How2Become Team

The police online assessment process is hard and stressful, which is why many good candidates fail it. This is why we have set up a dedicated, live webinar, presented by David Bebb, a Police recruitment expert with 30 years of experience in the MET. Our comprehensive assessment centre coaching will improve your chances of passing by increasing your knowledge, preparation, and confidence.

> - **INSIDER RECRUITMENT TIPS** to ensure that you pass your police assessment, first time;

> - **PROVEN INTERVIEW TRAINING** including how to tackle the competency-based interview questions and our winning template to form top-scoring answers;

> - **ACCESS PRACTICE RESOURCES** so that you can prepare for the College of Policing online assessment process;

> - **GET YOUR QUESTIONS ANSWERED** by a Police recruitment expert, with over 30 years of experience in helping people, just like you, to become police officers;

> - **LIVE TRAINING FROM YOUR HOME** via your PC, MAC, tablet, or smartphone to ensure you get the very best coaching available & your questions get answered.

Book your place now and get 10% off using the below code.

10% OFF CODE: H2BOAP10

www.PoliceAssessmentCourse.co.uk

Printed in Great Britain
by Amazon